Nell Hannah
Aye Singin an Spinnin Yarns

Nell Hannah

NELL HANNAH
Aye Singin an Spinnin Yarns

by
Margaret Bennett
&
Doris Rougvie
(Illustrator)

Grace Note Publications

Nell Hannah: Aye Singin an Spinnin Yarns
first published, 2013 by Grace Note Publications C.I.C.

Grace Note Publications
Grange of Locherlour,
Ochtertyre, PH7 4JS,
Scotland

books@gracenotereading.co.uk
www.gracenotepublications.co.uk

ISBN 978-1-907676-40-6

A Grace Notes Scotland project funded by
Heritage Lottery Fund and the Gannochy Trust

Grace Notes
Scotland
Handing on Tradition

www.gracenotescotland.org

Dedicated to all who hand on traditions

Acknowledgements

This book is part of a Grace Notes Scotland oral history project, 'The End of the Shift', funded by Heritage Lottery and the Gannochy Trust. The aim of the project is to record the experiences of folk who worked in past industries of Perthshire and East Fife, such as mills, dye-works, glass-works, factories, quarries and mines and to create books and educational materials as well as a dedicated website. This book is the first of these resources and we are very grateful to our funders for their support.

Special thanks also go to the staff at the Stanley Mill Museum for welcoming our visits, to Historic Scotland for permission to photograph the mill where Nell Hannah once worked, and to the ever-helpful staff at the A.K. Bell Library in Perth.

LOTTERY FUNDED

The Gannochy Trust

CONTENTS

SONGS

PHOTOS

Introduction

For over thirty years Nell Hannah has been singing songs and telling stories that are rooted in her own life. As she reaches her ninety-third birthday (2013) she can look back on a life that never had her utter the words, 'I'm bored.' More likely she'd ask, 'what's that?' And, as anyone who has spent time in her company knows, hours spent with Nell can evoke a world of memories that have lit up hundreds of folk. Getting involved in the oral history project 'The End of the Shift' gave us the ideal opportunity to record Nell, well known to the staff at Perthshire's Stanley Mill Museum as a former 'mill lassie'. Both children and adults who have enjoyed listening to her tell of her time as a 'drawer' in the mill will have discovered that life was not all work and no play. Even although the shift could be twelve hours long, and getting up at 5.30 a.m. was normal, yet Nell's generation describe a way of life that not only documents the social history of their time, but also brings reflections of their parents and grandparents. The details they remember are not the sort of information we find in history books, but the day to day reality of those who experienced it, and whose spirited attitude had them singing songs and spinning yarns that last longer than their years of hard work.

In today's media-driven world of consumerism, phrases such as 'I was a drawer' or 'I worked in the still room' might well evoke images of a trendy artist or a tranquil workspace. The notion of 'working for a fee' might attract attention of would-be executives who'd like to get on the ladder of ambition. And if the mention of 'the end of the shift' signals plans of meeting friends, a night with the feet up or maybe a bit of a spree, then meeting someone like Nell Hannah will add a whole new meaning to life.

In setting out to make oral history recordings for 'The End of the Shift' going to visit Nell Hannah was the ideal place to start. Doris Rougvie first met her at the Glenfarg Folk Club in the mid-eighties and for many years both of us have enjoyed sharing songs with Nell. Having heard her introduce her songs with colourful anecdotes of working at the mill convinced us that 'somebody should record her.' Happily the opportunity arose and we also invited young folk to take part. Four students of Scottish music at the Royal Conservatoire of Scotland volunteered, Ainsley Hamill, Sarah McNeil, Imogen Poropat and Robyn Stapleton. Not only did they all revel in Nell's company but also Sarah used some of the material in a student research project and singers Ainsley and Robyn now perform some of the songs Nell sang to them.On one of Doris's recording sessions she was in the company of Stuart and Gillian Duncan of Red Barn Recording Studios (Dundee), who filmed the session and gave Doris a copy to use for this book. We would like to thank those who helped with the final version of the book: Jim Douglas, Nancy Nicolson, John Hannah and Ewan McVicar for permission to print their song compositions, 'My Mither Milked the Turra Coo' (with drawing), 'Who Pays the

Piper', 'One Spare Kiss' and 'Shift and Spin'; Gonzalo Mazzei for typesetting, layout and design; Phillip Hannah for the cover photograph, and Hugh Hoffman for proof-reading. Nell herself would also like to thank all her family and a wide circle of friends, starting with Michelle who not only helps with transport but also goes the last mile in every way. Lest someone is inadvertently missed out, there is no list of names, but Nell accords her heartfelt thanks to each and every one.

Notes on fieldwork methods, editing and production

The entire book is based on oral history interviews with Nell, which Doris and I recorded over several visits. We began with the three of us present, then, as time and opportunity allowed, we would go back individually to add to the collection. The recordings themselves are now on digital files and so that they will be conserved and available for education and research purposes. They are deposited in the Perth and Kinross Archives at the A.K. Bell Library in Perth and in the School of Scottish Studies Archive at The University of Edinburgh, (with consent forms completed by Nell and Grace Notes Scotland.) Excerpts will also be available on the Grace Notes Scotland website, which is devoted to the larger project, 'The End of the Shift', taking in the wider industrial history of Perthshire and East Fife.

Turning recorded interviews into a book requires a considerable amount of time and effort, from the initial indexing then transcription and finally editing the material. We have divided these tasks between us: Doris transcribed all the recordings verbatim then did drawings while I rearranged, supplemented and edited the transcriptions to produce the book. As far as possible I have tried to keep Nell's own wording, particularly for anecdotes she related. Inevitably there were instances where information seemed to be missing so I would phone Nell, ask her more questions, take notes and then use the components parts to create a text that flows as a continuous narrative. To avoid disturbing the text with additional information (such as notes on song origins), end-notes have been added fro readers interested in these details.

We would like to say a big 'Thank-you' to Nell for taking part in 'The End of the Shift' project. We hope that in sharing her memories she has had as much pleasure out of this as she gives to others while handing on traditions to new generations.

Margaret Bennett
Grace Notes Scotland,
Comrie, 2013

Early Days

Iwas born in Turriff on June the 8th 1920. My father's name was Joseph Josephs, so I was Nellie Josephs. It's a Welsh name, because my father was Australian with Welsh parentage. My mother was Nellie Ledingham Young an she met my father during the First World War. He was an ANZAC an he came across from Australia as so many soldiers did.[1] After they married they lived with my mother's folk – in those days, an even after the Second World War when there was a real housing shortage, it was common for young folk to begin married life sharing the home with parents. My sister Margaret was the oldest,

Aunt Susan (left) with Nell's Mother, Perth early 1950s

then me, the middle one, an we had a baby brother. Sadly, though, I never did know my father because he left us when we were children.

I always felt the miss of not having a father an I always wondered about him, but my mother never spoke of him to us until the year before she died. It was Christmas Day an she took a funny turn so we put her up to bed an she said, "I've nae been a bad mither tae ye have I?" Then she said, "Your father was eleven years older than me…" An that's the first time she ever spoke about him – she told us what happened, another woman was involved…

My grandfather said, "Carry on with the marriage but if you do, you leave my house." So she had to choose between him an her parents, so she chose her parents – this is what happened. Sad, wasn't it? An we never saw him again.

So I was brought up in Turriff with my Granny an Granda in the house next door to St. Ninian's Church, at 23 Church Street, which is still there even although there have been a lot o changes in the town. In those days there were folk in Turra who even kept cows an it was all farms round about. My mother was a dairymaid wi a family called Tocher – the byre was in Market Street next to the poorhouse. She was away out five o'clock in the mornin so we hardly ever saw her, unless it was a school holiday. Then I used to be up in the loft lookin down at my mother milkin the cows, about ten of them. An she sent me down one day to try an milk, but the cow kicked me an that was the end of me wantin tae milk the cows! But my mother was good at it – she used to take part in the Turriff Show where there was always a competition for the best milker – she never got first but she always got second for milkin. They used to sing while they milked because the cows liked you to sing to them. They all had names – I remember her pet name for me was Kirsty because one of her cows was called Kirsty!

I went to Turriff School an we had this music teacher, Harry Green, a big man an I was petrified of him. An when I was about eight years old, he stood me up beside the piano one day an he said, "Sing!" An he started playing scales an of course I didn't really know what was expected an he told me to go away, I was hopeless. So I always thought that I couldnae sing, but it didnae bother me in any way – maybe I was relieved to be out of his way. I never tried to sing, but my mither had a beautiful voice. She sang 'The Bonnie Lass o Ballochmyle' – it's a Burns song:

The Bonnie Lass o Ballochmyle[2]

Fair is the morn in flow'ry May,
And sweet is night in autumn mild,
When roving in the garden gay,
Or wand'ring in the lonely wild;
But woman, Nature's darling child,
There all her charms she does compile;
Even there her other works are foil'd
Even there her other works are foil'd
By the bonnie lass o Ballochmyle.
The bonnie lass o Ballochmyle.

Chorus:
The bonnie lass! The bonnie, bonnie lass!
The bonnie lass o Ballochmyle.

Oh, had she been a country maid,
And I a happy country swain,
That shelter'd in the lowest shed
That ever rose on Scotia's plain!
Throu weary winter's wind and rain,
With joy, with rapture, I would toil;
And nightly to my bosom strain,
And nightly to my bosom strain
The bonnie lass o Ballochmyle!
The bonnie lass o Ballochmyle!

Chorus:
The bonnie lass! The bonnie, bonnie lass!
The bonnie lass o Ballochmyle.

Another beautiful song she used to sing was 'Mary of Argyll'– I used to love to hear her sing that one:

Mary of Argyll[3]

I have heard the mavis singing,
His love song to the morn,
I have seen the dew-drop clinging
To the rose just newly born;
But a sweeter song has cheer'd me
At the ev'ning's gentle close,
And I've seen an eye still brighter
Than the dew-drop on the rose.
'Twas thy voice, my gentle Mary
And thine artless winning smile,
That made this world an Eden,
Bonnie Mary of Argyle

Tho thy voice may lose its sweetness
And thine eye its brightness too;
Tho thy step may lack its fleetness
 And thy hair its sunny hue;
Still to me wilt thou be dearer
Than all the world shall own.
I have loved thee for thy beauty,
But not for that alone.
I have watch'd thy heart, dear Mary,
And its goodness was the wile
That has made thee mine for ever,
Bonnie Mary of Argyle

She had the sweetest voice, but she didn't sing a lot 'cause Mum didn't have much to sing about – she'd a very, very difficult life. So maist o my old songs were from my Granda. He used to sing to me as a wee girl, songs like 'Hey Johnny Cope are ye waukin yet an are yer drums a-beatin yet', but I can't remember all of that. Another one he used to sing was 'Watch her, track her, pipe her as she goes, high heeled boots an patent leather toes' and one of his favourites was 'I Met Her in the Garden Where the Praties Grow':

I Met Her in the Garden Where the Praties Grow[4]

Have you ever been in love, me boys?
Oh! have you felt the pain?
I'd rather be in jail, me boys,
Than be in love again.
For the girl I loved was beautiful,
I'd have you all to know,
And I met her in the garden
Where the praties grow.

Chorus:

She was just the sort of creature, boys,
That nature did intend
To walk right through the world, me boys,
Without a Grecian Bend.
Nor did she wear a chignon,
I'd have you all to know.
And I met her in the garden
Where the praties grow.

Said I, "My lovely colleen,
I hope you'll pardon me".
And she wasn't like the city girls
Who'd say "You're making free".
She looked at me right modestly
And curtsied very low.
"Sure, you're welcome in the garden
Where the praties grow".

Chorus:

She was just the sort of creature…

Says I, "My lovely darling,
I'm tired of single life,
And if you've no objections
I will make you my sweet wife.
" Says she, "I'll ask my parents,
And tomorrow I'll let you know
 If you'll meet me in the garden
Where the praties grow".

Chorus:

She was just the sort of creature…

Her parents they consented
And we're blessed with children three:
Two girls just like their mother,
And a boy the image of me.
We'll train them up in decency,
The way they ought to go,
And we'll send them to the garden
Where the praties grow.

Chorus:
She was just the sort of creature...

Granda he was a highland dancer too – he used to do 'The Highland Fling' with his tackety boots on the kitchen floor. And my Granny was a lovely wee woman, I was awfy fond o my Granny – she told great stories. She came from Cuminestown – Margaret Whyte had been her name, an she had been a cook to a doctor. I remember her mince an tatties an skirlie, an her barley broth, all done on the coal fire. An she always had a plain black apron for the mornin, an a silk black ane fir the afternoon. If there was a thunder storm, Granny would have all the mirrors covered up, the windows all open an she'd be in the chair wi the apron over her head till the storm wis over. An she'd open both the doors so the lightning could get through the hoose.

She used to tell us all these stories about Fyvie, like the Mill o Tifty's Annie, Andrew Lammie, The Grey Lady in the castle – that's the ghost that haunts Fyvie Castle, I believe her name was Lilias Drummond. If I remember rightly, Granny told about this Laird o Fyvie – his wife had died under mysterious circumstances, they weren't very sure if she'd fallen or what, but she died under mysterious circumstances an then he re-married. An the story Granny told me was that on the night of the wedding wi the new wife, there was a sighing an moaning all round the corridors of the castle when the Laird went to bed with his new bride. An in the morning outside a window was carved in stone the name Lilias Drummond an nobody knew how that had happened because it was stonework an it was deep down into the stone her name was carved.

She used to talk about Mill o Tifty's Annie, an how her two brothers broke her back on the stable door. You'll know the song aboot what happened – I don't sing it myself but I've heard it often:

Mill o Tifty's Annie

At Mill o Tifty lived a man
In the neighborhood of Fyvie
He had a bonnie dochter dear
Whose name was Bonnie Annie

Lord Fyvie had a trumpeter
By the name o Andrew Lammie
He had the art tae win the heart
O Mill o Tifty's Annie...[5]

It's such a sad story – I was actually taken to the cemetery at Fyvie to see Andrew Lammie's statue where he stands blowing his trumpet. He went to war an when he came back an discovered what had happened, he died of grief.

An Granny used to tell us a story about Carnousie Castle. One of the rooms has a ghost, because, so the story goes, the lady of the castle had been unfaithful to her husband an he shut her up in the tower an left her

Carnousie Castle

to starve to death. This young boy managed to get food to her, an he was caught, an they're actually supposed to have hanged him. So he is supposed to be one of the ghosts as well. An then there's supposed to be a piper as well – a ghost who plays tunes.

These are the sort o stories my Granny would tell an we loved stories. A lot o the time folk would tell ones about what happened just last week, say, anything out o the ordinary happened, maybe some scandal or something really funny – they'd be talkin aboot it for years. One o the things that happened before I was born the incident wi the Turra Coo. My mither spoke about the Turra Coo for as long as I can remember, because she had worked as dairymaid at a farm called Macterry o Rea an that's where this white cow came from originally. It was sold to Paterson at Lendrum Farm afterwards, so ma mither actually milked the famous 'Turra Coo' – it was in the papers, of course, an mither kept these newspapers all those years. So for years an years I've heard about this.

It was back in 1913 when Lloyd George was in office he brought out an act sayin that farm servants had to pay insurance stamps.[6] This farmer in Turriff, Robert Paterson at Lendrum Farm protested that the farm servants were poorly enough paid without an added tax put on them an he refused to pay the tax. As well as bein a farmer he was also an auctioneer at mart in Turra, an a partner in the firm, the Johnston an Paterson Mart. Then one day when Paterson was away from the farm an the council came an took a cow in lieu of payment. They couldn't take it

The Turra coo being brought home (Press photo, 1913).

to the mart in Turriff 'cause Mr Paterson was one of the people who owned it, so they took it to Aberdeen to sell it, but the people in Turriff were so angry about this that they clubbed together an went to Aberdeen an they bought the cow for £14. An they brought it back to Turriff an tethered it in the square an some wit painted on the poor cow, on one side it said 'From Leeks to Lendrum' ('Leeks' being Lloyd George) an on the other side o the cow was 'Free, wouldn't you like to be me' They brought it to the market place an they decorated this poor cow with garlands an all sorts. There was pipers an all sorts of noise an the poor cow ran away an it was chased all over Turriff. There was three days trial an one of the witnesses was asked about what was he doing while the cow was running amok. He said, "Och, I was jist standin on the corner o Duff Street lauchin!"

Then Mr. Paterson an his cronies were taken up for causing an affray an there was a big trial it lasted for about three days because it caused a riot. I think it was one of the country's first demonstrations so of course it was in all the papers. Anyway, the poor cow ran away wi aw this commotion an folk chasin after, she ended up in the back court of the Black Bull Tavern. An for years after that you could buy china, aprons an everything wi the Turra Coo on it – souvenirs, like wee milk jugs with the tail for the handle an the cow's mouth for the spout.

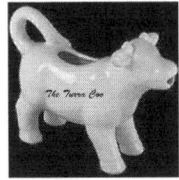

Years an years later after I'd been tellin this story, Jim Douglas wrote a song for me 'Ma Mither Milked the Turra Coo' – I'll sing for you later.

Jock Duncan & Doris Rougvie beside the Turra Coo Sculpture, 2013.
Photo by Hugh Hoffman, 2013.

Grandparents

We aye ca'd my grandfather 'Granda' an he was stone deaf though he actually wasn't born deaf. He had had a very bad accident in the harvest field when he fell on a pitchfork an the fork went right up his ear. He could be a grumpy old So-and-so, an he used to think if we laughed we were laughing at him. I think that's why I've got such a loud voice now, 'cause I used to climb up on his knee an roar into his ear, "I'm nae lauchin at you Granda."

Though he could be grumpy, he liked me, but for some reason he didn't seem to like my sister. He used to give me a Saturday penny, but I had to ask him for one for Margaret. We used to go into Smarts, this wee sweetie shop in the square in Turriff. I got a ha'penny worth o caramel bon-bons an a ha'penny worth o chocolate bon-bons. An I always brought back one caramel an one chocolate bon-bon back for my Granny. But one Saturday she was very angry at me. I had a friend who was from a big family an sadly their father had committed suicide an her mother was pretty poor so on a Saturday, she always sent her daughter down to the soup kitchen for a flagon o broth an plain bread. That cost a penny. So this time, when I got my Saturday penny, I went down wi her an I got a flagon o soup wi my Saturday penny an took it home. But Granny was so angry, because to her, that was

charity, so she got angry at me for spending my Saturday penny on charity, the broth. But eventually she felt sorry an ate the broth, because she probably realised I thought I was doing a wonderful thing for my Granny.

Another of my memories is when my Granny used to take us out visitin amongst her old cronies. We had a cuppie tea an I was told little girls have to be seen an not heard – that's what all children were told in these days. So we were at this Mrs. Cranna's this day, an Mrs. Cranna lost the teapot lid. An the two old dears searched about, an searched about for this teapot lid an I knew where the teapot lid was, I saw where she laid it down, but I couldn't tell them cause I'd been told I'd to be seen an not heard. Anyway, they gave up an just had their tea – she'd come across it later. An on the way home I told my Granny where the teapot lid was, an then I got a row for no tellin them!

My sister Margaret was a couple o years older than me, so I was the youngest in the family until one day we discovered we'd a wee brother so I was really the middle one. We had no idea we had a brother till he was five years old – somebody up in Macduff was looking after him an he'd had an accident. I'd've been about eleven an I remember them bringing John home with his head all bandaged. He was about five – that was the first I knew I'd a brother. He stayed with us after that an went to school wi us.

Sometime our cousins came up from Glasgow for a holiday an they'd stay wi us – the same house in

Church Street. Of course it wasn't very big, so we would sleep toppy an taily in the bed. An one horrible thing I remember in that house is one time when they were on holiday we were sleepin on this sofa down the stair an I put my feet to the floor this morning an the whole floor was covered in cockroaches – hundreds an hundreds of them, cockroaches! I've never forgotten that. We got 'Keatings Powder'. But mind we were clean people, it wisnae that we were dirty – they'd come doon the pipes.

We always went for a walk on a Sunday afternoon after Sunday School an we didn't think anything about walking several miles because we were used to it, our legs were pretty strong. Sometimes we used to picnic at the Pinkie Braes an in spring it was full of primroses. It was lovely when we all went an my mother could come too – you remember these warm, sunny days. The Minister's Den was also a place where you could get lovely flowers, lilies an things. Anyway, this Sunday my sister an I were on our way to the Pinkie Braes an 'The Minister's Den'

We loved to go for a picnic on a Sunday, but I mind that day a horneygollach went down the back o my frock! That's Mother drinking her tea, second from the Right. (Turriff, early 1930s).

is down that road, about five miles from Turriff, down the Banff road. If you go over the Deveron Bridge, where the bridge is there's a little toll house. But on this particular walk we finished up at Carnousie Castle which was against the rules – that's the one in Granny's story. But we were told never to go there, no because o the ghosts but because my cousin had a school chum who was drowned in the river there an we were told it was out of bounds. However, we went there, we wandered into the grounds of the castle, an there were lovely lilies – that's what we called daffodils an narcissi – I still do. An it was a lovely day so we were pickin the lilies an then we sat down to enjoy the sunshine. But who should come along but this gillie? An having just been to Sunday School we were wearing Panama hats wi plenty room in them – you had to wear a hat to church in those days, you wouldn't dream of going to church without a hat! So we hastily put the lilies in our hats an put our hats back on over our heads. An he said 'You're no supposed to be here, bairns.'

We sort o nodded. He said 'Ye hinna been pullin the flo'ers have you?'

We shook our heads, an he said "There's the gate! Skoot! Get hame!"

Years an years later, we thought on that when my cousin Iris's son, Colin Baxter bought Carnousie Castle! (He's a skin specialist in Canada.) There we were, welcomed in the front gate, an treated like royal guests for the day. It was a whole lot better than being thrown out the back gate as bairns!

Turra in the Twenties an Thirties

The travellers, or tinkers as we always said, would always come round. People depended on them for mending farm implements an making pails an jugs an things – some of them were real experts but of course they didn't all work at tinsmithin. We liked to see them comin an Granny was always good to the tinkers, they always got a cup of tea at our house. An one of them used to play the trumpet, he'd be buskin oot in the street, playing jazz an all sorts of things. As children we were all out in the street when he used to come, an everybody gave him pennies. Then he always came into our house an blew the trumpet into my Grandfather's ear. Afterwards he always got his cuppie tea an a couple o pennies. Mind, you could do a lot wi a penny in those days.

In the town there was what they called 'the common ludgin hoose'– some real characters stayed there, like an old man we knew as 'Forty Pooches'. He wandered about Turriff in all weathers an people gave him their old coats. They called him Forty Pooches because when he got another coat he never took the old one off, he just put the new one on top. So he had forty pooches an the kids used to make fun of him. Another o his nicknames was 'Harry Humpy' because he used to shuffle along an all the kids thought it was great fun to shout at him. I remember wee Jackie Chalmers saying, "Let's call him

Harry Humpy an he'll gie's a chasey!" I discovered a long time afterwards that this man had worked on the railway an he'd been crushed between buffers, so he'd got a big compensation. When he died he left a lot of money yet he lived in the ludgin hoose. He was one o the worthies o Turriff, I remember well. In fact one o the boys at school wi me made a poem about aw the worthies that bade in Turra – 'Auld Turra Cronies' – I don't think I've got all of it, but here's most of it:

Auld Turra Cronies[7]

There was Sinclair the mason on cricket real keen,
Simon the Cobbler tae mend yer auld sheen,
Davie Rennie fae Fife Street wid sell yea stirk,
An Christie the draper wha sang in the kirk,
Carnegie the Butcher wi his broon Shalt an float
An Steven the tailor tae mak ye a coat;
An auld Briggie Wallace wi kye an a tyke
An Dickie fae Gray Street tae mend yer auld bike;
There wis Lord Kintore fae the Tap o the Toon
An Circus Neddie tae gie you a tune;
There was John Low the plumber, an Bob his mate
An Blackie the painter near the kirk gate
Miss Knox at the laundry wid iron yer sark
Adam Dreamer the painter sang like a lark;
John Robb the baker wis good at the ba'
But Samson the Miller wid gie nothin' awa.
Frank fae the Howe wi his fob an his chain,
There's Lyle the teacher, real good wi the cane;
The mason James Robb wi his level an square,
Willie Thain, he's the poacher – that's him ower there;
There was Melville the draper wi chokers real deep

An auld Jock Philp wi his horse an his wheep
There wis Esslemont the tailor, wi new hoose sae braw
An Ewan the jyner tae shairpen your saw
There wis auld Murray Gillan wha shauchled gey sair,
The dummy fae Haughs an Jimmy gey mair
There wis Mason the butcher, Hughie Grant aye had tea
An Gammie the Baillie wi a wink in his ee,
Oot catchin poachers he'd walk mony a mile,
An Baron, the hiring, bade nichts i' the jyle
There wis auld Jessie Sentor at the White Horse
An gunner Mill cam fae the Big Key at the Cross
The twa Meldrum sisters, Francie Kelman the painter,
Dallas fae Fife Street, Melven the baker
Auld Jessie Renton, noo she was real quick,
The first wi the news an wi gossip real slick
She could tell te fa's deed an fit's tae be born
Fas wifie's run away, an fa's mairyin the morn;
At politics quick was Leithem the printer
Willie Grieve fae Ashogle, now he wis a thinker;
There wis Kelman the scaffie wi his shovel an cairt
Shan the draper, wi claes sae smairt;
Jimmy Marr, fae the Marrs, he'd mend your auld grate.
An Inglis the Chemist, his pills keep ye straight;
At Broon's shop Harry Riddel, wi his hat on his lugs
At the mart, Maggie Pirie fed the men an their dugs;
Jumper Watt wi his bell goin' roon' wi the news
Shoutin "Oh yes! Oh yes!" A'm awa, too-ra-loo!

I canna mind them all but Leithem the printer, he wis the
Provost for many years an he was also editor for 'The
Squeak', *The Turriff Advertiser*. Willie Thain the poacher, he
kept ferrets an one day when I wis playin in the gairden wi
Bunty Thain, his granddaughter, when Willie came home

drunk. He thought it was a great joke to put a ferret doon my back. Well I screamed an screamed, I can assure you I alarmed the whole neighbourhood wi my screams! There was something too about auld Francis Harper – I saw him in his coffin, when my Granny took us to see him. That's what they did in her time. I mind when Frank Kelbie died, he was the one wi the fob an chain – the Kelbies were scrappies an Frank wis the grandfather, a big fat man, an he always had his watch chain across his tummy. There were a few scrap metal merchants, families who dealt in the 'rag an bone' trade, the MacAlisters, the Kelbies an the Gillespies who lived in Mill Street, the Howe o Turriff, what they used to ca the Howe o Hell. I mind when Frank Kelbie died they had a four day wake for him.

My Granny used to take me to visit 'The Poor Hoose' One of her friends was a Mrs. Maitlan who had the 'Poor Hoose' in Market Street an I remember sittin in this room, an all round the walls was box beds. An in the box beds were old people in white goons. That was the 'Poor Hoose'. Now that's some memory isn't it?

It may have been everybody's dread that they would 'end up in the poor house', as that was the only option

of food and shelter available to those unable to look after themselves – under the same roof were the poor, destitute, feeble in body or mind, lunatics, the elderly and frail, without any family to help them. Set up all over the country in accordance with a series of Poor Law acts passed from 1834 onwards, these poor houses became landmarks in many communities. There were also Model Lodging Houses, especially in the cities, where there was accommodation for families or single labourers who could not afford or find housing. From early Victorian times till the middle of the twentieth century, they were a familiar form of social service, or 'parish relief'. Not surprisingly, children learned from a very early age that "if you don't work you won't eat."

Poor, but never hungry

My Granda was quite a character in his time. He was a market gardener – the onions I saw on the telly put me in mind o the ones Granda would grow. Have you heard o the Haughs in Turriff where they have the Turra Show? Well Granda's garden had five levels right down to the Haughs, an my mother faithfully dug this garden for ten years till he had to sell it – my mother wasna pleased about that because it was such a godsend, an she'd have loved it, but he said he had to sell it to pay the grocer's bill. That's was the way it was then, you'd have an account in the shop till you had money comin in to pay for it, but sadly if you didna, you'd have to do your best to settle any debt.

But when we were still at school Granda's vegetables were fantastic an his rasps were some size. An we used to pinch them but we could never understan how he knew – of course he'd know by the husks that were left on the bushes! I used to get the job of helpin him to get the vegetables ready for the 'Turra Show'. I remember scrubbin the onions, an the carrots were huge. An I used to have to help him push the barrow down to the school, where the show was. One year he swept the boards – twenty-one entries an twenty-one First Prizes!

The winter nights were great fun because Granda used to sort all his shallots oot, an he put them in drawers. An when it came to eating them, he used to take the shallots oot, put them into the fire an then get the tongs an pull them out an we'd eat them. They were delicious, roast shallots.

He grew beans an he'd get me to help when he'd bring in lots an lots of beans home, the big white ones an he used to boil them. Granda an I were the only two in the house who liked them, an I used to get bowls full o these. There's one thing, we might hae been poor but I don't think I was ever hungry when I was a child. My Granny kept hens so we aye had eggs an we sometimes had a chicken on a Sunday.

Working hard did not always mean that the wages earned would feed a family – they might scrape by on that, but, when it came to putting food on the table and making sure nobody went hungry, the best fed were families who grew their own vegetables. Throughout the year folk also knew what was in season and where to gather wild foods, freely available in fields or along pathways and lanes. Nothing could be harvested or gathered, however, withoot considerable effort – as the old folk were fond of saying, 'Naethin is gotten withoot pains or hard work but an ill name an lang nails.'

Granny's kitchen

In the spring granny used to make nettle soup wi the new nettles – it's delicious. It's not just that the nettles are free but they're really good for you. She used to make  wine with the nettles as well, an in the late summer we'd pick rosehips an she'd make jelly. In the autumn folk would be picking brambles along the roadside or whatever happened to be ripe – there were lot of things you could pick an everyone just knew what they were an how to use them. My Granny wis a great wee wifie. She had been cook to a minister an she was a wonderful cook. We had a coal fire wi a swye that we hung kettles on, an she used to cook on this open fire. Her mince an tatties were great an her barley broth.

She had a brander across the top o the fire, a metal things like a griddle, it went on top o the fire an it had a handle for lifting it on an off. An two old fish wifies used to come up from Macduff every week, Mrs West an Mrs Lyons, wi creels on their backs, an Granny always gave them a cup o tea. We used to get yella fish an it went on the brander – the fire had to be just right, with glowing embers that sort of seared the fish – it was beautiful.

Of course you'd always have to clean the fire irons an such. But that was one thing I didna like was cleaning the fender. I used to get the job of cleaning the fender wi Zebo – that's what folk used to clean the grate.

Another meal we used to get wis 'Hairy Tatties' – a bit like fish cakes, made wi dried speldings, dried fish. When you got them fae the fish-wife they were like boards so you would put them in water to soak them overnight. When you boiled them the texture was like hair. An she'd boil a pot o Granda's tatties, an then mashed up the tatties an fish thegither – you could see then why we called them 'hairy tatties' an they were great. You always had them wi mustard sauce an oatcakes of course.

One of the things my Mither did to make money was to make oatcakes for people. She made the most brilliant oatcakes an she had an iron thing on the front o the fire for the oatcakes to toast, they curled up. We used to get what we called the raw oatmeal – the real oatmeal, we always got this. You can still buy it, though in those days folk would get a hundredweight bag to last for months.

The poorest people ate sowens an sautie bannocks – it was the standard in the old days when people were poor. Sowans was made from the meal husks. when the corn's winnowed – that's what it's made with. It's steeped in water an it ferments, then it's boiled up and gets thick like a porridge. You only come across it in songs these days, like 'The Twa Recruitin Sergeants'[8].

The Twa Recruitin Sergeants

Twa recruitin' sergeants cam frae the Black Watch,
Tae markets and fairs some recruits for to catch,
An aw that they listed was for forty an twa,
Sae list my bonnie laddie an come awa,

Chorus:
For it's over the mountains, an over the main,
Through Gibraltar to France and Spain,
Get a feather tae your bunnet, and a kilt
    abeen your knee
An list bonnie laddie an come awa wi me

It's intae the barn and oot o the byre
This greedy auld fairmer thinks that
    you'll never tire
It's a slavery job o low degree
Sae list bonnie laddie an' come awa wi me.

With your tattie poorins an yer meal an kale,
Yer soor sowan soorins an yer ill-brewed ale,
Yer buttermilk, yer whey, an yer breid fired raw.
Sae list my bonnie laddie an come awa.

Oh laddie, ye dinna ken the danger that ye're in,
If your horses wis to fleg an' your ousen wis to rin.
This greedy auld fairmer winna pey your fee,
Sae list bonnie laddie an' come awa wi me.

O laddie if ye've got a sweetheart an bairn,
Ye'll easily get rid o that ill-spun yarn
Twa rattles o the drum aye and that'll pay it aw
Sae list my bonnie laddie and come awa.

There can scarcely be any aspect of farm work that does
not have some song about it. Nell was scarcely aware that,
as she listened, the words of the songs stayed with her,
particularly 'old favourites' she first heard at home. But,
much as her mother loved singing, she was often simply

*too exhausted from what seemed like endless work. She
longed for the day her children were old enough to leave
school and find a job so that things might be easier for all
of them.*

She'd a very, very difficult life an Mum didn't have much
to sing about. She worked for this family called Tocher,
as I said, milking the cows twice a day an doing seasonal
work forbye. She used to get a job at the mill at the
harvesting. She was on top o the mill an we used to
think it was great, we used to take their pieces out to the
people an we'd sit in the ricks wi the soup an things. We
used to play hide an seek in the ricks, the stooks o corn
when she'd be on top o the mill, tyin stooks. But when
she came home at night she'd be almost fainting with the
thorns under her nails. Sometimes they'd be way down
the side o her nail-bed an I used to get the big darning
needle to take these thorns out o her fingers. I was only
a wee lassie but I remember it well. An there wis an awfu
lot o rats an I remember my mother catching them in
these great, big metal cages that were for catching rats.
They would trap about ten rats at a time an my mother
would drown them.

Thankfully there were occasional highlights in the year, especially during the festive season or the end of the harvest when the community would enjoy time to sing and have fun.

When we were children Christmas was wonderful. My Mother had this friend in Kendal, Mrs Ainsworth, whom she met her when my Father was in the Army an my Mother was down there too. Well, she was always very good to us at Christmas an we always got a parcel in the post from Mrs Ainsworth. An I remember one parcel, it was baby dolls wi china faces, just like babies. My sister an I just loved them! An on Christmas Eve we always hung our stocking up at the fireside, by the mantelpiece an we'd be so excited! It was great wakin up on Christmas morning an going downstairs to the fireside to get our stockins. An in the toe there was always a sixpence, a handful of nuts, an apple an an orange an a wee dolly. An we always got a pair o socks or something like that, to wear. That was our Christmas stocking an it was wonderful for us, we couldna be more pleased because we didnae have much you know – nobody had much so Christmas was a real treat.

Christmas and New Year

We always had our Christmas Soirée at the church. Someone would always han out a bag to us as we went in the door – we got the paper bag an inside there was always a cookie, a cream cookie, an currant bread, an we got a cup o tea, but I never ate that currant bread – I always took it home for my Granny. She loved it so Granny always got the bit o currant bread for a wee treat.

When I was five, there were four of us all dressed in nightgowns wi our teddies an I was supposed to go on an sing this song but unfortunately beforehand, I unexpectedly met Father Christmas in the corridor an I screamed the place down. I'd never seen him before, an he seemed such a great, big man, an I was terrified of him. My mither said she was black affronted because Father Christmas came on the stage carrying me in his arms. When I recovered I sang. An I've remembered that ever since... I can still see me in that nicht-goon, on that stage singin that song.

How'd you Like to be a Baby Girl?[9]

Oh, good evening, pray how do you do,
We are babies come to sing to you,
Cheeks like roses, hair that's all in curl,
How'd you like to be a baby girl?

34

When Father Christmas brings you lots of toys,
Dolls to cuddle, drums to make a noise,
Skipping ropes an spinning tops that twirl
How'd you like to be a baby girl?

When the doctor, spectacles on nose
Feels your pulse an says 'Well I suppose,
Water, castor oil is the best dose,'
How'd you like to be a baby girl?

Another year I remember Dr. Bruce helping me on wi my wellies. I must have been about six or seven. My Grandmother was in the audience an of course so was ma mither. An I remember I was wearing a dress that had arrived in one of these wonderful parcels from ma mither's friend in Kendal – cast-offs, I expect. You can imagine how thrilled I was that one of the dresses was this beautiful lemon silk one with little rosettes all round the waist with different coloured ribbons hanging down. It was a beautiful little dress an there I was, looking a picture in it an I was reciting this poem. I can't remember the words of it but it was a poem about a wee girl who'd gone out on her granny's birthday an – it was composed from the point of view of the wee girl, as if she was telling what really happened. So there was I, I'd found eggs an

I'd brought them in, in a basket an put them on a chair, an my granny sat on them. It turned out to be a clutch of thirteen eggs an I shouldn't have touched them – a hen would have been, you know, sitting on them. My Granny told us afterwards that there were two country wifies sittin in front o her an one looked over an said, "That's a bugger o a lassie, that!"

They were believing the poem – they were believing that it was me! That was my performance when I was a little girl.

Hogmany was a special night, of course. An in Turriff, the big corn meal store, Hutcheon's, had great big gates that were always kept closed. But on Hogmany night all the kids went down an stood outside the gates an we all sang:

> Rise up guid wife an shak yer feathers
> Dinna think that we are beggars
> We're only bairnies come to play,
> Rise up, an gie's oor Hogmanay.
> Wir feet's weet, wir sheen's thin,
> Gie's a piece, an let's rin,
> Yir purse is fou o money,
> Yir bottle's fou o beer,
> Gie's a bawbee tae bring in the New Year!

Then at midnight, at the bells, the big gates were opened up an all the kids in Turriff went there an we got an apple, an orange an we got sweeties. An then we would go up to Stewart the Bakers an we'd get mince pies there – they were all good to us. It's all changed now, the kids couldna do that because it's dangerous, but in those days there was no danger goin out at night. Folk didna need tae worry.

Childhood Games and Rhymes

Aw the kids played outside when they weren't at school or helpin their parents. It was a healthy way of life because were aye outside, wi lots o games like 'Hoist the green flag' – that was a tracking game where started from the 'bed base' an you took a piece o chalk an arrows in certain places all round Turriff. The idea was to get back to the 'bed base' without being caught an when you got to base without being stopped you shouted 'Hoist the green flag!' That could take half the day! It's not played everywhere because years later I got a job at a holiday camp in in Lowestoft an I had all these kids running round the camp making arrows an shouting 'Hoist the green flag!' They thought it was great fun but I haven't seen it for years –kid's don't do that now, it's too dangerous. On these nights when dusk was falling in Turra we were perfectly safe going about the streets.

The school had a good playground, girls on one side an boys on the other an at playtime we loved to play peevers. You'd always get a wee piece o chalk to draw the beds – when the chalk was too wee for the teacher to hold, she'd throw in the bucket an get a new one. When you went out to the bin to sharpen your pencil you could aye pretend you dropped it in the bucket

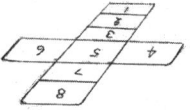

then pick it out a wee bit o chalk when you bent down to pick up the pencil!

We played 'Giant Steps' – that's when one person stood with their back to everybody an they'd say so many 'giant steps' an you'd have to do exactly that before the person would turn around an catch someone movin. They would say 'Three giant steps', but if they just said 'Three steps' an you moved, you were out. It's like 'statues' – that's another game where you were out if you were caught moving.

We played 'What's the time Mr. Wolf?' an we also invented games. I remember one time when Mr Kelman's canary died we had this funeral for it. Children didn't really go to funerals but we'd seen them often enough so we had a service for the poor wee canary. We got a wee box for the canary, the coffin, an we all dressed up. I was the minister an for some reason I was wearing somebody's longjohns! Then we had a funeral procession for this canary, through the streets, an eventually we buried it in the garden.

Children everywhere played in the streets because there so few cars, so it was quite safe. When you saw a lorry or car comin you'd just clear out the way. When someone had a bouncy rubber ball, we'd sing an play:

> One, two, three a leary,
> I saw Mrs Peerie
> Sittin on her bumbaleeree
> Eatin chocolate soldiers.

An we'd be singing an makin up dances, heel toe, heel toe, to go wi the song:

Charlie Chaplin went to France
To teach the ladies how to dance.
First the heel an then the toe,
That's the way the polka goes.

Another game we used to sing was 'That's the style of the army'. It was an action song an everyone had to start off in a circle, singing:

When Captain Jinks comes home at night
He claps his hands with all his might
He looks the part, got up so bright
For that's the style of the army.

Then you'd change to doing the actions for each verse, like 'Join hands':

All join hands an forward all,
Backwards all, backwards all,
All join hands an forwards all,
For that's the style of the army.

When Captain Jinks comes home at night
He turns his partner on his right
He turns his partner so polite
For that's the style of the army.

Promenade around the room,
Around the room, around the room,
Promenade around the room,
For that's the style of the army!

I don't know where we heard them, but we had lots o songs an games, an aw the kids would know them.

When I worked as a Children's Hostess at Kessingland Holiday Camp near Lowestoft, I used to teach the children the games we played as bairns. (late 1950s).

Entertainment

There used to be a travelling company who came to Turriff an put on productions, little theatre pieces, like 'Mill o Tifty's Annie', 'The Red Barn' an 'The Mains'[10] an 'The Mains Again'. It was a farming story, about farming people – 'The Mains' was one, then 'The Mains Again'. An what else was there now? Oh, a wonderful Gilbert an Sullivan group, I don't know where they came from but they must have toured village halls an the likes. We would see things like 'The Mikado', 'The Pirates of Penzance', all these things. I always managed somehow to get the money to go to these things. They'd pack the hall – the Town Hall in those days, charging a bob, or mebbe one an six. So I was brought up wi the music – a lot of music. The Scouts put on great concerts, an the Sunday School had 'Soirées' as they called them. Everybody would go to the Kirk Soirée.

There were films too – an to begin with it was silent movies, an they played the piano for the silent films, but then we got the talkies, we got sophisticated! We loved going to the pictures – that cost a penny, an was in the Town Hall. An one o the first films I ever saw wis 'Ben Hur' – silent – an of course there was Laurel an Hardy. Then when ye got to be twelve, ye graduated to pay tuppence, ye got up in the plush seats an 'talkies'.

In May an November, Whitsun an Martinmas feein

time, Turra would be packed – folk came from all over, farmers an workers lookin for a fee. They hid all sorts o stalls in the market place in Turra an they hid a fair wi the showds. D'you know what a showd is? It's the swing-boats, they called them 'showdies' an they also hid a roundabout. One year they had Rose Darling (she was a gypsy fortune-teller) an Speedy Sedgewell on The Wall o Death. I remember getting an awfy row fae ma mither 'cause Elsie Kelman an I were up in the parkie as we called it, Rose Darling came up to us an asked us if we could look after the children in the caravan while they were on the wall. Oh her caravan wis lovely, the glass an silver, an absolutely immaculate of course. Ma mither wis angry at us mixin wi people like that – what stupid ideas she had about that kind of thing.

In our street there was a family called the Kelmans – we were one end o the block on Church Street an they were at the ither end o the block. An out at the back we had coal sheds an that's where we used to go in an tell stories, sing songs like 'Polly-wolly-doodle all the day'. An they had this old gramophone, a cylinder – they used to play songs you know, Al Jolson, things like that. Oh, we had songs in school too, like 'Barbara Allan', 'The Auld Hoose', 'The Flo'ers o the Forest', all the standards. But I wisna very much involved in singin at school because, mind, thon Mr. Green said I couldna sing. But it didna stop me listenin or joinin in.

We had an old gramophone, a wind up one, an one of the songs that stayed in my mind an was brought back to mind one Sunday when I was listening to Robbie Shepherd on BBC Radio Scotland. He spoke about this song, 'Will the Angels Play Their Harps for Me?' An the minute he mentioned it I had complete recall from the old

78s. We used to listen to this old wind-up gramophone and play the same records over and over and this was one of them. An on the other side of that record was 'The Wanderer's Warning'. Years an years later I sang it at Milnathort Festival – it's supposed to be a sad song an by the time I finished singing it we were in hysterics, the tears were running down my cheeks. I can still sing it yet!

The Wanderer's Warning[11]

Oh boy, hear the wanderer's warning,
Don't break your poor mother's heart,
Stay by her side for she needs you
An let nothing tear you apart.

I cursed an swore at my father
I told him his words were a lie;
I caught up my things in a bundle
An went to bid mother goodbye.

My poor mother broke down crying
"My son, oh my son, do not leave!
Your poor mother's heart will be broken
An all her life long she will grieve."

I cursed an swore at my father
I told him his words were a lie
I caught up my things in a bundle
An bid my poor mother goodbye.

Childhood was a training ground for hard work but it ended all too soon for Nell's generation. The official school leaving age was thirteen and few youngsters had the opportunity to go on to college or university, far less stay on in school any longer.

I had to leave the school when I was thirteen an a half 'cause there was no money you know. This was 1933, the 'hungry thirties' an my mother needed us to be working – my sister had already left home an gone into service – that's what my mother had done when she was young, so we had to do the same thing. When I started, my wage was five bob a week, yes, five shillings a week[12] working as a domestic servant. It was a terrible life because I had to live with, an work for the messiest old woman who shouldn't have had charge of a child you know – an I was just a child. When I had to do the washing I had to light boilers to get the water hot, an doing the washing it was a bit of a nightmare, I'd be terrified of getting burnt.

A couple o years on, the farmer's wife wis expecting a baby an I wis sent to help out at this farm. I'd only be fifteen, I was hired as a kitchie deem an like the other farm servants you lived on the farm. I'd a bed up in the loft so it wis pretty basic. I don't think the farm servants had much o a life. One o the things the boys loved to do wis torment the kitchie deem, an I never had a life really 'cause I got tormented by the lads – an I have scars to prove it. What happened was, on November the fifth they hid a great Guy Fawkes Nicht, a great procession through Turriff – just bands an things like that you know. Everybody came out in the streets so of course we were there. Well, they let off this jumpin cracker, an Wallace Grant, who was one o the bothy lads at the same farm as me, he kicked it an it landed up on my knee, an I still have the scars to prove it. I'll tell you something, though, my mother wis mair mad an mair worried aboot my coat than aboot my knee, because there wis a hole burnt through the coat!

That was nearly as hurtful as the sore knee. Anyway, that same Wallace Grant also thought it was great fun when I used to go an feed the hens because he knew that when you'd go up the cornlaft there wis this big rooster an he went for you, because it wis his territory. An he'd be worse if there was clockin hens. So when I went up there this big rooster would go for me an I wis petrified – he wis a big heavy bird you know.

Well, Wallace wis on top of a haystack an he said to me next time you go up that cornlaft take your bucket an go "Shoo!" But he knew full well it wouldnae deter this cockerel in the least. Well, ower this bird came, an I'm goin "Shoo! Shoo!" an it came all the faster. So I turned tae run, an it landed up on my back, an you know they have big spurs. An Wallace fell off the haystack laughin. But I got my own back, 'cause I had to make the beds in the bothy, an I put thorns in them – the chaff beds they had were gey lumpy, tickin on top, well I pit thorns in them. Anyway that was life as a kitchie-deem. Not glamorous in the least.

I would have done anything to get away from that place. You know the farm workers were so poorly fed the only time they got a bit o beef wis probably on a Sunday. They used to go an catch rabbits so they could get stew. They hid brose in the mornings – pease brose, or neep brose, aye that's jist the juice o neeps, mixed up wi oatmeal. That's what we used to live on. We didnae get fed well. An the problem wi them was, they had to fee on for six months, 'cause they took the shillin, they took the 'arles', at whit they called Porter Fair. That wis the feein time – the farm servants came in an went to Porter Fair, the farmers were there an they would approach a bloke an ask him "Are ye needin a fee?"

An if he said he wis, the farmer would gie him a shillin. An once he gave him that shillin, it wis an unbreakable contract for six months, he couldn't leave. So if he went to a farm where they wernae fed, they'd a hard time. Mind you there wis a sort o grapevine – if it wis a poorly fed farm, word would be passed round: "Dinna go there 'cause it's no fed very well."

That wis life. An being a kitchie deem certainly wisna for me. Mind you, I still like the songs we used to sing, an they really do tell what it was like on some o these farms, the hirin fair or fee'in market as they called it.

The Barnyards o Delgaty[13]

As I ga'ed doon tae Turra Market,
Turra Market for tae fee,
An I met in wi a wealthy fairmer
At the Barnyards o Delgaty

Chorus:
Liltin adie toorin adie,
Liltin adie toorin ae,
Liltin lowrin, lowrin lowrin,
The Barnyards o Delgaty

He promised me the twa best horse,
That ever wis the country roon
But when I got intae the Barn Yards,
There was naethin there but skin an bane!

Chorus: *Liltin adie...*

The auld grey mare lay on her hunkers,
The auld din horse lay in the grime;
An a' that I could humph an cry,
They wadna rise at yokin time.

Chorus: *Liltin adie...*

Meg MacPherson maks ma brose,
Her an I can ne'er agree,
First a knott, an syne a mott,
An aye the tither jilp o bree.

Chorus: *Liltin adie...*

When I gang tae the Kirk on Sunday,
Mony's a bonnie lass I see,
Prim, sittin by her faither's side,
Winkin ower the pews at me.

Chorus: *Liltin adie...*

The candle noo it is brunt oot,
The snotter's fairly on the wane,
Sae fare ye weel ye Barn Yards,
Ye'll never catch me here again.

Chorus: *Liltin adie...*

That was a great song for getting everyone to join in
the chorus – I mind hearin the Joe Gordon Folk Four
singin it on one of these old 78 rpm records. Then in the
Sixties they used to have 'Bothy Nichts' on Grampian TV
– everybody used to look forward to that. And in those

days if you didn't have a telly, and a lot o folk didn't, you'd go next door to watch wi the neighbours. It was great way o getting folk together an everyone joinin in.

And another o the songs that you'd hear then, was Nicky Tams – that's one by George Morris. But of course in our day all the boys an the men who worked on farms wore nicky tams. They'd tie them round their breeks just below the knee to keep them out o the wet an the mud. An of course they'd keep anything from crawling up the leg o their breeks.

Nicky Tams[14]

When I wis barely twelve year auld
    I left the pairish school.
Ma faither fee'd me tae the Mains
    tae chaw his milk an meal.
First I pit on ma narra breeks
    tae hap ma spinnel trams,
Syne happit roon ma knappin knees,
    a pair o Nicky Tams.

Well, first I gaed on for baillie's loon
    an syne I gaed on for third,
An syne, of coorse, I had tae get
    the horseman's grip an word.
A loaf o breid tae be ma piece
    an a bottle for drinkin drams
Ye daurna gang throu the cauf-hoose door
    wi'oot your Nicky Tams.

The fairmer I am wi the noo
    he's wealthy but he's mean.

Tho corn is cheap his horse is thin,
    his harness fairly deen,
He gars us load oor cairts ower fu',
    his conscience has nae qualms.
When breist-straps brak
    there's naethin like a pair o Nicky Tams.

I'm coortin bonnie Annie noo,
    Rab Tamson's kitchie deem,
O she is five an forty
    an I'm but seeventeen,
She clorts a muckle piece tae me
    wi different kinds of o jams,
An tells me ilka nicht that she
    admires ma Nicky Tams.

Ae Sunday mornin I gaed oot,
    the Kirkie for tae gang,
Ma collar it wis unco ticht
    ma breeks were nane ower lang,
I had ma Bible in ma pooch,
    likewise ma book o Psalms,
When Annie roars 'Ye muckle gype,
    tak aff yer Nicky Tams!'

So, unco sweer, I took tham aff,
    the lassie for to please,
But aye ma breeks they lurkit up
    aroon aboot ma knees,
An a wasp gaed crawlin up ma leg
    in the middle o the Psalms.
O never again will I rade the Kirk
    withoot ma Nicky Tams.

Noo, I've aften thocht I'd like tae be
   a bobby on the Force.
Or mebbe be a tramwayman
   an drive a pair o horse.
Whatever it's ma fate tae be,
   the bobbies or the trams,
I'll ne'er forget the happy days
   I wore ma Nicky Tams.

McGinty's Meal an Ale[15]

This is nae a sang o love, na
   nor yet a sang o money,
Faith it's naethin verra peetifu',
   it's naethin verra funny;
But there's Hielan Scotch, Lowlan Scotch,
   butterscotch an honey,
If there's nane o them ava,
   there's a mixture o the three.
An there's nae a word o beef, brose,
   sowens, sauty bannocks, na
Nor pancakes, Pace eggs
   for them wi dainty stammicks;

But it's a' aboot a meal an ale
    that happened at Balmannocks
At McGinty's meal an ale,
    whaur the pig ga'ed on the spree.

Chorus:
They were howlin in the kitchen
    like a caravan o Tinkies, aye,
An some were playin ping-pong,
    an tiddely-widdely-winkies
For up the howe an doon the howe
    ye niver saw such jinkies,
As McGinty's meal an ale,
    whaur the pig ga'ed on the spree.

Noo McGinty's pig had broken lowse,
    an wannert tae the lobby,
Whaur he open shived the pantry door,
    an cam' upon the toddy;
An he took kindly tae the stuff
    like ony human boddy,
At McGinty's meal an ale
    whaur the pig ga'ed on the spree.
Miss McGinty she ran but the hoose,
    the wey was dark an crookit,
She ga'ed heelster gowdie ower the pig,
    for it she never lookit;
An she lat oot a skirl
    wad hae paralysed a teuchit,
At McGinty's meal an ale
    whaur the pig ga'ed on the spree.

Chorus: *They were howlin...*

Johnnie Murphy he ran efter her,
    an ower the pig was leapin
Whan he trampit on an ashet
    that was sittin fou o dreepin
An he fell doon an peel't his croon,
    an quidna haud frae greetin
At McGinty's meal an ale
    whaur the pig ga'ed on the spree.
An the pantry shelf cam' ricklin doon
    an he was lyin kirnin
Amang saft soap, pease meal,
    corn floor an yirnin
Like a gollach 'mang trickle
    but McGinty's wife was girnin
At the soss upon her pantry fleer
    an wadna lat him be.

Chorus: *They were howlin...*

Syne they a' ran skirlin tae the door
    but fan that it was tuggit,
For aye it held the feester,
    aye the mair they ruggit;
Till McGinty roared tae bring an axe,
    he wadna be humbuggit,
Na, nor lockit in his ain hoose,
    an that he'd lat them see.
Sae the wife cam' trailin wi an axe,
    an through the bar was hacket,
An open flew the door at aince,
    sae ticht as they were packet,
An a' the crew cam rummlin oot
    like tatties frae a backet,

At McGinty's meal an ale
    whaur the pig ga'ed on the spree.

Chorus: *They were howlin...*

They had spurtles, they had tattie-chappers,
    faith they werena jokin
An they swore they'd gar the pig claw
    whaur he was never yokit
But by this time the lad was fou'
    an didna care a dockit
At McGinty's meal an ale
    whaur the pig ga'ed on the spree.
Oh! there's eelie pigs an jeelie pigs,
    an pigs for haudin butter,
Aye but this pig was greetin fou'
    An rowin in the gutter,
Till McGinty an his foreman
    trailed him oot upon a shutter,
Frae McGinty's meal an ale
    whaur the pig ga'ed on the spree.

Chorus: *They were howlin...*

Miss McGinty took the thing tae heart,
    an hidit in her closet,
An they rubbit Johnnie Murphy's heid
    wi turpentine an rosit;
Syne they harl't him wi meal an ale,
    ye really wad supposit
He had sleepit in a mason's trough
    an risen tae the spree.

Oh! weary on the barley bree,
    an weary fa the weather,
For it's keetcherin 'mang dubs an drink,
    they gangna weel thegither;
But there's little doot McGinty's pig
    is wishin for anither
O McGinty's meal an ale
    whaur the pig ga'ed on the spree.

Chorus: *They were howlin...*

After a spell o workin on the farm in Craigston, outside Turra, I went to Aberdeen to work, still in my teens. I went into service first an then I got a job at the Caledonian Hotel in Union Street, as the still-room maid – big houses an hotels an castles all had a stillroom where they keep the jams an jellies, bottled condiments, pickles an various bottles o beverages. When I started there, it was filthy so the first thing I did was to clean it up – the boss couldna believe the difference! I didn't live in, so I had to get digs an of course I'd look forward to getting home for holidays. But when I came home at Christmas-time my mother had taken a job at the egg depot where they used to pluck turkeys an birds for the Christmas season. She was the head plucker an when I came home ma mither would be in the pluckin sheds, wi a' these wifies were sitting there wi the crates o hens an geese an ducks an turkeys an chickens – they were all in boxes, crates like, an you would just reach out for one an wring the bird's neck. An I had to help ma mither, killing turkeys – you'd do it wi a big stick across their necks an you put a stick on the ground over their necks. An then you took a hold of their wings an when they pulled themselves back to try to get away, they killed themselves, broke their own necks. Of course getting them under the stick wisna easy an my legs would be black an blue from the ankles up to the knees – I'd be eighteen or nineteen, an when I look back on that episode I canna believe I did it. Aye, I can still see ma mither sittin there, an all these women pluckin fowls aw day. I wis doin that with her when I was home on holiday, an we got tuppence for a hen, fourpence for a duck, sixpence for a goose or a turkey.

This day lorries came in wi a load o turkeys for the depot an some o them were so overcrowded that a lot o the birds were bruised so they couldn't sell them. They still had to be killed an plucked even though they weren't really fit for selling, but all the pluckers were offered the chance to buy two turkeys for half a crown each! In the days of food rationing this was too good to miss, so we got the two turkeys, wi not a thought of how we'd cook them. We were living in this wee, wee house in Watt's Lane in Turriff an we had a gas boiler for washin clothes an that's what we cooked the turkeys in. In the boiler, the gas boiler! An we invited all the neighbours in, an everyone had turkey an tatties an neeps. It was a tiny little room you know, an we'd a house full o people, wi everybody enjoyin the turkey – cooked in the washin boiler! Ah, the things you had to do in those days, but it was just a way of life, nobody thought anything about it.

Of course Christmas was a great time for folk to get together an there would always be folk who sang. An we used to listen to records on the wind-up gramophone – an if there was a new record out an somebody bought it then everyone would hear it so often you'd learn the songs. There were some really great singers, real old favourites like Willie Kemp an George Morris – they wrote a lot o these songs[16]. Maist o the old songs I remember now were from my Granda, who used to sing. This is one that Granda sang, but I only started singin it years after he died.

The Buchan Bobby[17]

I am a Buchan Bobby
    an my name it is McQueen.
I wis born an bred in Buchan,
    syne I cam tae Aiberdeen.
Hoo I cam tae Aiberdeen
    I'll noo tae you relate,
But afore I tell my story
    the truth to you I'll state.
My mither mends my auld breeks,
    my faither ca's the ploo.
A but n' ben wis a' oor hame,
    we'd fodder for a coo.
The smell o ham an eggs an beef
    it never reached wir nose.
I wis brocht up doon in Buchan,
    aye, an maistly on the brose.

Chorus:
'Flat feet! Bap feet!'
    hear the bairnies cry,
Early in the evenin
    as I'm passin by.
Keekin roond the corner
    shoutin 'Here he goes!'

But ye canna touch the Buchan lad
*   'at's fed upon the brose!*

Ah fee'd an wis contentit
    till I wis near nineteen;
I wis second lad at Hillie's
    far we hid a sauncy deem.
I fell in love wi Nancy
    an speired gin she'd be mine,
But she said she widna hae me
    altho she liked me fine.
She said, 'Man, Ah like ye Geordie,
    but Ah'm scunnered o this life
A cotter's life's a trauchle,
    so if you want me for your wife
You'll hae to try some ither job
    as Ah tellt ye weel yistreen.'
So that's the wey Ah jined the force
    an cam tae Aiberdeen.

Ah wis pitten oan the nicht-shift
    an drafted tae Queen's Cross,
Ah felt a bittie awkward
    an sometimes at a loss
Fan the servant deemies cried me in
    an gied me the glad eye,
But Ah wis ayewise true
    tae Nancy milkin Hillie's kye.
Ah saved an scrapit ilka merk
    an hed a holiday
Gaed aff tae see my Nancy
    sae happy an sae gay
But fin Ah got to Hillie's

Ah could scarce believe ma een,
She'd gaed aff an mairrit the second lad
   an cottared at Kilbleen.

Ah felt so lonely standin there,
   that I could only stan an stare,
My Nancy noo I couldna see,
   sae lonely I wid hae tae be
In the toon o Aiberdeen
But Ah pull'd maself thegither,
   I dinna cry or yell
There are quines in Aiberdeen,
   so she can gang tae far-iver she likes!

Chorus:
'Flat feet! Bap feet!'
   hear the bairnies cry,
Early in the evenin
   as I'm passin by.
Keekin roond the corner
   shoutin 'Here he goes!'
But ye canna touch the Buchan lad
   'at's fed upon the brose!

It fair puts me in mind o when I was workin in Aiberdeen – stayin in digs, makin new friends, goin tae the dancing an all that. When you remember the fun you don't think so much o the long hours an hard work. I was there when war broke out in 1939 an that's when I met Harry – he was from Hull, an course I wasn't to know then that this was the man I'd later marry.

Harry was a fisherman an at the beginnin o the war he went into the Merchant Navy. An like the rest o the

Hull fishermen he came up to Aberdeen because the port of Hull was closed. So I met him there, we met in the same digs in Aberdeen. I thought he looked like Jimmy Stewart (the actor) when we first met – he was nine years older than me an I thought he was wonderful. We went out together but I always remember we were at a party one night an there was a woman who made a dead set at Harry, so I was kinda peeved! An bein young an petulant, I stormed out from the party I went home to Turriff – to cool down or to let him see I wasn't havin anyone mess me about. Anyway, away I went, an there was a terrible snow-storm. It didna take me long to have regrets about reacting like that, but when I wanted to go back to Aberdeen the train wisna runnin because of the snow. An by the time I got back into Aberdeen, Harry's ship had sailed an he was on his way to Norway. I thought I'd never see him again because we didn't even exchange addresses – he only knew I lived in Turriff.

Harry Hannah
Aberdeen in 1939.

Moving to Stanley

By that time my sister an I had both left home an my brother was in Turriff with my mother, who was still workin day in, day out. But the next thing we knew, Aunt Aggie, my mother's sister, who lived in Stanley became ill with cancer an my mother decided to go down to look after her – she lived in Russell Street. So my sister Margaret an I moved to Perthshire to be with my mother an my brother joined the Navy – at seventeen he went off to serve his country. We packed all our belongings an loaded them an ourselves on to a lorry an travelled in the same lorry to our first home in Perthshire, Waterloo, a wee place half a mile north of Bankfoot.[18] It was a cottage where another relative had lived an it had no running water – we got our water from a stream, which ran through the garden. An to do our washing we filled a big pot outside from the

Stanley Hotel

Stanley Mill, 2013.

stream an we lit a fire under it to heat up the water an rinsed our washing in the stream. The following year, I celebrated my twenty-first birthday in that cottage, June the 8th, 1941.

We got jobs in the Stanley Mill, all three of us, an the mill bus used to pick us up in the mornin at half past five to take us to work – it was like a mini-bus an it used to go through Bankfoot an round all these wee villages every mornin. Then we moved into a mill house in King Street next to the Stanley Hotel. It had a coal fire for cooking, a wash-house and, horror of horrors, a dry lavvy. Having come down from Turriff in Aberdeenshire we had a flush lavvy, even if it was up the garden. But you soon get used to it an I took to workin at the mill like a duck to water! Having had to leave school an go into domestic service as I did, I felt a sense of freedom working in the mill. I could sleep at home every night an we got a half-day off on Saturday an all day Sunday.

It was a jute mill[19] an I got a job as a 'drawer' in the card room an so did my sister. Ma mother's job was pushin the bogeys of bobbins about the mill – a big change fae milkin cows, but she didn't seem to miss that one bit. She mighta missed Turra but more likely, she didn't miss the endless work she'd known all her life. When you have to milk cows, you still have to milk them on Sunday, so a day off was something she'd never known an neither did I till I went to Aberdeen. When I think back, bein in service at thirteen an a half, at the mercy of some old women that today would be charged with child abuse – the way you were treated, an you got about five bob a week. I was always running away an my mother was always dragging me back saying, "If it was good enough for me it's good enough for you." She told the same thing to my sister but I'm afraid it wasn't for me. But I did enjoy working in the mill – it was like a new lease of life for me because you were free.

So we didna mind the early rises in the morning an mill bus would drop us all off at the gates, ready to start work at quarter past seven. The bell used to summon us to work an if you were still outside the gate when the bell stopped you had to stan out there for a quarter of an hour an they took thruppence off our wages if we were late. So we used to dash down an this bell going, I don't think I ever got caught anyway. There were about three hundred folk workin at the mill, an that was at all the different jobs. We started at quarter past seven in the morning an finished at seven at night with a half hour off for lunch. I was on piece-work an I think my top wages came to about two pounds fifteen shillings a week.[20]

When we started at the mill, we were told we would be making jute webbing – that's used for a lot o things, like the outside covering o fire hoses and conveyor belts and other things. They didn't tell us what the webbing we made was used for and we didn't question – we just made it.

From the time the raw jute arrived at the mill to when it left as webbing or whatever, there were all these stages. It has to be imported as it doesn't grow here, so it was shipped to Dundee from India and Russia. It was unloaded in big bales an it went to Perth an then to Stanley. You could tell the difference in the jute, though you'd have to work with whatever arrived – the Indian jute was OK but the Russian stuff was terrible to work with, horrible stuff. You had to piece the ends an it kept breaking. If it came from India you knew the difference, it was a better quality. An when these big bales o jute arrived they went into what was called the 'blow room' – they'd be taken apart an then all the impurities were blown out. There's a lot o different stages, wi different machines.

Then the raw material came up into the 'card room' – there were different machines on that floor for the different stages. Huge machines. First it went into carding

The toilet in the corner

machines, where it would be combed out an turned into continuous 'slivers',[21] like spirals of cotton wool. There were about twenty cans to each head of the machine, an when the jute had been put through rollers, through the cans at the other side, it was more refined. An these machines were behind my machine, the 'drawing frame', which was the next stage. The jute came to my machine in tall cans filled wi 'slivers' then I fed them through a series of rollers into the back of the drawin machine. My machine had three heads an the slivers were combined in a single stran an wound into more big cans.

An from there it went across to the slubbin frame an came out on bobbins an from there it went on to the 'roving frame', where it was slightly twisted before it was wound on to bobbins. The fibre has to have a twist in it so the strands will stay firm, like wool or cotton, you can see it has more than one stran or ply twist in the thread. An the people who worked on the roving frame had to build the bobbins up on their arm in a sort of pyramid an carry them from one frame to the other. To get the balance walkin with all those bobbins they always leant to the side, you had to, to carry them – you always knew who worked on the roving frames because, doing this all day long, they'd still be walkin to one side at the end o the shift.

After it had been through all that, the bobbins were ready for the spinning room where it was twisted again an wound more tightly on to bobbins. An the lasses who worked there had to move quickly as they'd go up an down a row of machines, repairing breaks an snags. An eventually it was ready for the weavers. Can you imagine the noise o all these machines an aw the dust, the stoor? It was so noisy we had to use sign language to communicate. You got an awful lot of fluff in your hair an you had an awful job getting it out of your hair. An we used to get jeely jars full of water handed round to drink. There was a wee toilet on each floor, in the corner, no room to swing a cat – there was a cold water tap, the same tap where we got our drinkin water – don't ask about hygiene.

An when you had to go, the gaffer would be timin you an that was awful. If you took any longer than five minutes you heard about it. At least the floors were bright, lots o windows, an in the card room, just behind me, the window looked right over the river an in the autumn I used to say, "I wish I could paint a picture of the colours in the stretch outside the window."

Of course nobody would be staring out a window! You really had to concentrate on your machine or you could lose a finger, but when you passed by the window you'd see out – an it's still beautiful. I think that lifted my spirits if they ever got low – just lookin out at the river an hearin the noise o the water. Maybe that makes it sound

View over the River Tay

glamorous but it was dirty an full of hazards – an it was how we made our livin.

Bein on piece-work, we wanted the belts to go quicker so we could make more stuff. We used to put this Grippo stuff in the wheel it made the big belts go quicker – it was like a block of amber an if you put it against the big wheels you could speed the wheels up. An the old gaffer, Davy McPherson, used to get on at us, an we were always being told not to do that. He'd say we could lose an arm an we just used to laugh. But years an years later I became a home help an I went into this lady's house, she was from Lancashire an she'd only one arm. I said, "What happened?"

She worked in a cotton mill an she told me she'd been doing the same thing that we did. "It was just like a big, loud bang!" she said, an her arm was gone.

During the war the mill was probably running at its peak – everything in those days seemed to be for the war effort an we were making jute webbing an things for the army though nobody told us that at the time. The funny thing about it is that I had never seen the finished product until I came to the Stanley Mills Museum to tell stories to children. An one day there was a box beside my chair an it was a water bottle with webbing round it. Till then, I'd never had any idea what we were making but it was soldiers' gaiters, belts an things like that. That was the policy in the factories – the workers wouldn't be given any information that might leak out – so we weren't told that we were making webbing for the soldiers. It's really strong stuff wi a very tight weave an it's used for belts in machinery, like conveyor belts and things. .

Years after the mill had closed down an became a museum, I went back, an the memories came flooding back. An the first time I went to the card room I sat there an remembered everybody's names an what they did in that card room. There was a great community spirit, which was one of the reasons I enjoyed it an the other was because I was getting to sleep at home. At the end o a shift you were back home wi your family an that was something I hadn't known since I left school at thirteen.

Visiting Stanley Mill

Nell visiting the Mill

Stanley Mill Gate

Stanley Mill Chimney

Looking at the Wheel Pit, Stanley Mill

Stanley Mill from the inner court

Tayside Hotel, once known as the 'Hen Hoose'

Wartime

During the war years with rationing in place things could be quite frugal but everyone accepted these restrictions. By the time we moved to Stanley everyone had ration books an fact it made folk more resourceful – you'd 'mend an make do' an there was these posters about 'diggin for victory', so people were plantin vegetables an growin things we'd always grown.

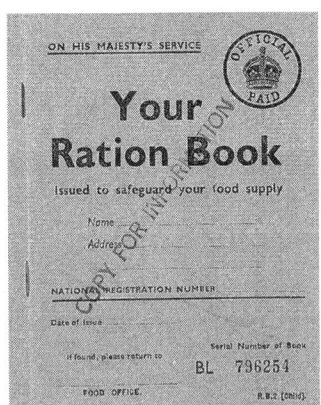

Ration Book
This image is from the collections of
The National Archives.
Reference: BT 131/40. WWII

An we used to do things, like mash up parsnips an pretend they were bananas. There was dried milk an dried eggs – that was a big change after growin up wi cows in Turra – an there were wartime recipes, but I can't say they were all a great success. That little house in King Street could tell some stories, like the time Harry was home on leave an I decided to make rissoles. It was all coal fires an we had a little Bunsen stove we sometimes used. You had to eke out your meat rations wi tatties an breadcrumbs an powdered egg an this was one of the recipes that was goin round. So I mixed them all up in the pan but it went into one horrible big mess. My husband was sitting there laughing so I threw the pan at him an it went flyin past him an up the wall. An there was my mother, scrapin grease off the wall, but fortunately we saw the funny side, an for years after, if ever I'd say "What are we gonna have for our tea, Harry?"

He'd say, "Rissoles!"

You didn't waste anything an though clothes were rationed too, you'd use any materials, like an old coat could be cut up an sewn into children's clothes. We even unpicked parachutes to make underwear an blouses. All the women's organizations used to knit socks or mittens an hats to send to the troops – the Red Cross especially would send parcels with these knitted things an a few goodies. They'd package them up an send out what they called 'comforts for the troops'.

There were soldiers stationed all over the place an of course my mother had an open door – she was great, she gave everybody cups of tea an all that. We always had a house full of soldiers an there was always a sing-song. An one day I looked out of the skylight when we were still in Turra, an there's this Welshman, Evans, comin up the lane. He came in to our house an he took this packet out of his tunic an it was bacon, they'd cut it wrong or something, so they got rid of it, an they brought it to us. Then we had the soldiers coming round an my mother cooked us all sausage an bacon – that was a treat when meat was rationed.

There was always something happenin, an folk would be trying to raise money for the war effort. We had a concert outside Watts Lane at the beginning of the war for the Spitfire Fund an my brother went round on a bike advertisin it. We had another concert in the Turra Mart an I was going round with lavender water to try an get the smell away! The provost was invited an he got a seat in the auctioneer's box an we had about fifteen Welshmen, soldiers – of course the Welsh are great singers, wi their fantastic male voice choirs. An after the concert they came to our wee house an they were singing 'Sospan Fach' an the mirror fell off the wall! I don't know how they all got in that wee place.

Believe it or not, we had a lot of fun during the war. There was such community spirit an great entertainment – if some folk tell you they enjoyed the war, that's what they mean. There were a lot o songs that just caught on and everybody knew them, of course the old war-time ones like 'Yes we have no bananas' and 'Mairzy Doats'. And one I used to love (and I still sing) is 'Let Him Go, Let Him Tarry' – it use to be played a lot on the wireless in the Forties:

Let Him Go, Let Him Tarry[22]

Farewell to cold winter, summer's come at last
Nothing have I gained but my true love I have lost
I'll sing and I'll be happy
   like the birds upon the tree
For since he deceived me I care no more for he.

Chorus:
Let him go, let him tarry,
*   let him sink or let him swim*
He doesn't care for me nor I don't care for him.
He can go and get another that I hope he will enjoy
For I am going to marry a far nicer boy.

He wrote me a letter saying he was very bad
I sent him back an answer saying I was awful glad
He wrote to me another saying
    he was well and strong
But I care no more about him
    than the ground he walks upon.

Chorus:
Let him go, let him tarry...

Some of his friends had a good kind wish for me
Others of his friends they could hang me on a tree
But soon I'll let them see my love,
    and soon I'll let them know
That I can get a new sweetheart
    on any grounds I go.

Chorus:
Let him go, let him tarry...

He can go to his old mother now
    and set her mind at ease
I hear she is an old, old woman,
    very hard to please

It's slighting me and talking ill
  is what she's always done
Because that I was courting her great big ugly son.

Chorus:
Let him go, let him tarry…

When I think back on these wartime years, folk got on with each other an they made an effort. They helped one another an really there was a great social life when we were workin at the mill in Stanley. We got Saturday afternoon off an all day Sunday so we'd take a bus into Perth on Saturday afternoon an our first stop was the Playhouse. We had tea in the Playhouse Café an in the evening we went to the theatre, up in the gods for sixpence. That was during the time of the great Marjory Dence an David Steuart. Can you remember these people? Oh they were well known.[23] I remember plays like 'Lady Windermere's Fan an 'An Ideal Husband' (both by Oscar Wilde) an I'll never forget 'Mary Rose' by J. M. Barrie. An I saw Lesley French in 'Ghosts' – that performance haunts me to this day.[24] We heard big bands like Joe Loss an laughed at great Scottish comedians such as Tommy Morgan, Dave Willis an Walter Carr to name a few.

A lot o the lassies I worked with used to go to the dancin – we loved the dancing an of course there were some fantastic players you couldn't miss. In spite of the long hours we worked, myself an seven other friends left Stanley, took Blair's taxi to follow Jimmy Shand, Adam Rennie, Ian Powrie an Ian Cameron all around Perthshire. The taxi set us down at the door. Now this could be a Friday night an you'd have to get back home again an still be ready for your work in the mornin!

We sometimes went twice a week if we heard they were playing in one o the villages. An more than once the taxi broke down in the middle of the night an had to be rescued! One night we didna get home till nearly five in the morning an we still got up in time for work – it was worth it!

There's one late night I'll never forget. I used to go to York House, that was another dance venue in those days, an I went there one night an met a dashing French Canadian called Arman Deloria. We danced together all evening an when the dance finished he said he'd walk down to the bus with me, an I said OK. There was a little fish an chip shop in Kinnoull Street, 'The Oasis', so he said, "Would you like some Fish an Chips?"

I said, "Oh yes."

So we stopped in 'The Oasis', ordered our fish an chips, but it came out just in time for us to see the last bus for Stanley going round the corner! Of course I was very dismayed about this an he offered me his room in the Salutation Hotel. But I said, "No, I can't do that my mother will kill me, I've got to get home."

So I started walking up Dunkeld Road an I met a lady coming down with a little Scottie dog, so I gave her my story an she kept saying, "Oh that's awful," an *she* offered me a bed for the night.

But again, I said, "Oh no, I've got to get home my mother will kill me!"

After a short while, along came a motorbike with two men on it an they stopped so I asked them for a lift. Petrol was one o the first things to be rationed durin the war an they said they could take me as far as the smiddy, just outside Luncarty, but I'd have to walk from The Three Brigs. When I think of it now, what a risk I was takin just to get home for fear my mother would angry! Anyway the driver was up in front, the pillion passenger up the back an I sat in the middle – I was like a bean pole in those days, could you imagine, so there was room for all three of us. An it's a cold drizzly November night an I've a vivid imagination an every time the bike went over on it's side, I'm thinking I'm going to be found dead in a ditch in the morning. But we got to Luncarty an they dropped me off an I walked the rest o the way. It was about four o'clock in the morning before I got home, an my mother was really angry. I told her what happened an when I said he's coming out tomorrow to see that I'm all right, she said there would be no bloomin foreigners comin here! But when he did come out to Stanley he was treated very well. It happened to be my cousin Alan's birthday, he was home from the navy, so he shared the clootie dumplin with us. Then he said to my mother, "There's a Polish concert in the Alhambra tomorrow night, could I take Nell?" (Nellie I was in those days).

My mother said, "Yes but she'd better be home an not miss the last bus this time!" So he took me to the concert an we went round to get the bus an we were so worried in case I wasn't going to get home, I shut the bus door in the poor man's face an I never saw him again. His favourite song was 'If I Were a Blackbird' an some time later when I was having my daughter in the maternity ward, they were playing Johnny Canuck's Review on the wireless an who should I hear but Armand? And he was whistling that song, 'If I Were a Blackbird'. That was a real old favourite an I still sing it.

If I Were a Blackbird[25]

If I were a blackbird, I'd whistle an sing
An I'd follow the ship that my true love sails in
An on the top riggings, I'd there build my nest
An I'd pillow my head on his lily white breast.

I am a young maiden an my story is sad
For once I was courted by a brave sailor lad
He courted me strongly by night an by day
But now my dear sailor is gone far away

He promised to take me to Donnybrook fair
To buy me red ribbons to tie up my hair
An when he'd return from the ocean so wide
He'd take me an make me his own loving bride

His parents they slight me an will not agree
That I an my sailor boy married should be
But when he comes home I will greet him with joy
An I'll take to my bosom my dear sailor boy.

I remember a great dance in Kydd's Rooms in Dundee. Some o the dances were quite formal, like this dance-hall. An I had a black evening dress with spangles down the sleeve – I felt right posh you know. My pals an I got into this particular set an we thought some o the other dancers were awfu snooty. Anyway we'd started this dance 'There's Nae Luck aboot this hoose' – you cast off an all the ladies come down the middle. An this time, there we were comin down the middle an this lady comin down with me seemed to hesitate. An I thought, "What's she doin?"

An she said "Ye're awa wi my hairnet!"

We all had a laugh an after that there was nobody snooty – we had a ball, a great time, an we got hot bridies at the end of the evening afore we went home.

The Scottish Country Dance Society met in the Salutation Hotel in Perth every Thursday so I joined that. Our teacher was Miss Mary Scrymgeour, headmistress at Caledonian Road School, an we always felt we were still her pupils when we danced anywhere. She taught us very well, so much so that years later when I went to live in Lowestoft I was able to start my own class, teaching Scottish Country Dancing.

The dancin was where a lot o folk would meet their partners – some o the girls met their husbands at a dance but that's not where I mine. I'd already met him in Aberdeen but of course thought I'd never see him again. As things turned out, the Stanley Mills played cupid in my life because this is what happened: The mill was taking thruppence from our wages every week for 'comforts for the troops' an if your brother or your husband or someone in your family was in active service you could mention you'd like them to get a parcel. An the secretary, Sue Graham, said to me one day, "You've never given us a name of someone you'd like to receive a parcel an you're paying us all this money every week."

I says, "Well I do know somebody I could send a comforts package to, but he doesn't know where I am." An the only reason I knew where Harry was because, just by chance, a friend of his sent me Harry's address in Norway. So then I gave Sue Graham the name anyway. About a fortnight later she was goin past my machine an every time she passed my machine I thought she gave me a funny look. I wondered, "What's she lookin at me like that for?"

So it was a while after that I went home one day an my mother said, "There's a letter for you an it looks like Harry Hannah's writing."

I said, "Don't be daft Mum," but when I opened the letter, so it was! He'd got this comforts package, which just said "from Stanley Mill" an he told me afterwards that he thought the only person who would think enough of him to send him a parcel was me! So he'd written to the mill an asked for my address an that's why Sue had known what was going to happen.

So anyway he got in touch an said he was going on leave an could he come an see me. So I told my mither, Harry wants to come, an very grudgingly she said, "Oh I suppose so."

He came an he stayed with us for a week an nothing was said about getting married that time. But he was home on leave again, that was 1942, an he'd been there a couple of days an he said, "Don't you think we've wasted enough time already, what about we just get married?"

So we went an called the banns we were getting married an people were astonished they didn't know I had a boyfriend at all.

The people who worked in the mill couldn't get time off, not even for your own weddin, so I had to get married in the evening. The day I left to get married, at the end o the shift the lassies dressed me up wi a big hat wi flowers on it, they put a big 'L' on my back, for Learner, an stuck a bunch o flowers in my hands. I carried a chamber pot full o salt wi a wee dolly sitting in it – that's what they used to do. Then they put me in the bogey, a mill bogey, like the one my mother used to push, which had metal struts. An you see those round pillars on the carding room floor, like columns? Well, off we went, an every column we came to they went crash into them! Talk about a commotion, the girls laughin an there's me, sayin, "It's gonna be my funeral!"

The next day I was black an blue an I could hardly move, wi them bumpin into the pillars wi the bogey, but we had great fun.

We were married in the manse, my wedding suit was a utility outfit[26] an my hat was a pillbox with a long feather. My brother dropped the ring an we spent ages searching for it under the settee for it. When the minister said, "You can kiss the bride" I nearly knocked Harry's eye out wi the feather! An we had eighteen people sat down to a meal. We had hired benches an tables from the bakers an we had mince an tatties, trifle an clootie dumpling. I found the bill some time later an it was twelve shillins an six-pence for eighteen people.[27] Of course there was no icing on the cake an no camera so we never even got a photo of my wedding.

What I didn't know at the time was that Harry was going to Russia. He knew where he was going to go, but he couldn't tell me that because everything had to be kept secret. An so not long after we were married he was away – an he was in Russia for six months. I was still staying on King Street with my mother an Margaret so not a lot changed at home because– that was the way it was during the war, you just had to carry on as normal.

On Sundays we went to the Free Kirk on Mill Street an my sister an I joined the Free Church Women's Guild. An one time when the Guild had organised a 'Basket Tea' for the Spitfire Fund in St Columba's Hall, we wrote a script for the entertainment.

We were also in the WRI – the 'Rural' we used to call it (Women's Rural Institute) - The women got together and had all kinds activities like making things to send to the troops.

They were also very keen on Amateur Dramatics. So this time Margaret an I wrote a script an when the audience arrived we told them they were all going to be part o this play – they were all supposed to be hostellers an I was the Warden o this hostel, Mrs Alistair MacAlistair. The hall filled up an among the audience was the manager o the mill an we gave him a part too so he'd be joinin in wi the rest o us. An there was a group o us who went to the Scottish Country Dance classes, an these dancers were also to take part. Anyway, the night began: There was a knock at the door an in came Mr Hutton (the manager of the mill) with eight country dancers. They said "We're 'The Scotch Broth Concert Party' an our bus has broken down so we need beds for the night."

And, bein the warden o the hostel (in the skit), I said "Oh, great we'll have a ceilidh after tea!"

So this ceilidh begins an the first act of the evening was to be 'The Life an Times of Bonny Prince Charlie an Flora MacDonald.' An there were Polish soldiers in the audience an though the Poles didn't have a lot of English they knew something that we didn't know about Bonnie Prince Charlie – his mother was a Polish Countess.[28] After the concert the Polish captain came to see me an asked us to repeat it for them, an invited the audience, the whole of Stanley, down to Campsie Linn for a Song-Sing as they called it. They had an orchestra playing Strauss waltzes an they had a choir that sang 'Over the sea to Skye' in English – the Polish soldiers had learned this in English. It was quite a night an I think that everybody from Stanley was there.

The Polish soldiers used to go to the local dances too – some really lovely young men. Before I was married I walked out with one once or twice – Jan was his name, an we were walking out Perth Road one afternoon when the hawthorn was in bloom. He clipped the hawthorn off the tree, dusted the road with his hanky an knelt down an presented me with it. Wasn't that romantic? But there's one dance that sticks in my mind because it really was quite funny. I'd just been married about three months an Beth McKerecher an I were at a dance one night. An Beth was married as well an we danced wi these two Polish lads. Then we spent the whole evening dancing wi these two Poles an when it came time to go home we were a bit worried. It was blackout of course, so we decided we'd try to sneak away through the cloakroom, so the girls took the blackout off the window an put me through the open window an I fell on gravel on my knees an ripped my stockings. Then Beth an I ran all the way home an apparently the two Poles were standing at the gate waiting for us when the dance finished. About a week later I got on the bus in Perth an there was only one seat left, an that was beside this guy that I'd run away from. I sat down an he said, "Why did you run away?"

I said, "I am married."

An he said, "I am married to a girl in England, but this is life." Then he said, "British girls are very cold but you get to thirty an you change!"

There were so many soldiers everywhere, British soldiers as well, of course. An in 1942 we had a number of soldiers billeted in the hotel next door, the Stanley Hotel. It was harvest time an when some o them were working in the fields my mother would have some of them in for cups of tea. An one day, these officers knocked on the door an one o them said, "Are you the lady who gives my batman cups of tea?"

I thought we were going to get into trouble but he said, "My batman is in the harvest field," – presumably the batman would have made the tea for him, an he introduced himself. This was Colonel Duncan an he had just come up from Dundee an would really love a cup of tea so I asked them in an made tea. An the colonel was sitting reading *The Courier,* an he said, " Our troops have landed on Anzio beach an Colonel Duncan is having a cup of tea in Stanley."

A week later I got a little parcel an when I opened it, there was ten bars of Duncan's hazelnut chocolate – he owned the factory in Dundee!

That was a real treat during rationing – some o the girls at the mill used to pool our sweetie ration, an then once a month or so we'd go across to Hancock's an just gorge ourselves on sweeties. An fruit was scarce too so the only people allowed oranges were pregnant women. I went to the Co-Op one day when I was expecting my first baby, an it was August Bank Holiday, an the manager said, "Haud your bag open," an he poured about fifteen Jaffa oranges into my bag. When I went home, we had a feast of oranges.

My first baby was a wee girl, Thyrza, born in 1942 when we were staying on King Street. The Italian prisoners of war were next door to us in the Stanley hotel an they were billeted in the wooden building, like an annex, at the back of the hotel. There were about fifty of them with one Irish sergeant in charge, an Paddy was his name. Thyrza would be about 18 months old this particular time, an I had three friends who also had babies. The three of us, young mothers, walked every day wi the bairns, out to what they ca 'The Two Trees' an I remember one beautiful day we were goin for a walk, so I got Thyrza's little bonnet on an her nice little dress. She was a wee picture an I put her out in the pram an went inside to get myself ready. When I came out the pram was gone, the baby was gone! An of course my first child, I was in a right state! I ran down the brae to see if maybe some child had pushed the pram down the brae, but no, so on the way back I was on my way to contact the police an could hear laughter coming from the back of the hotel. But of course the building where the Italian prisoners were was out of bounds to villagers, so I had no right to go round there, even though the place was attached at the back of our cottage. So I went round the back, as any mother would, an there's Thyrza sitting surrounded by about ten smiling Italians! They'd been feeding her chocolate an it was all over her face an her little dress an even her sunbonnet. They were saying, "Bambino, bambino," so delighted to see this child, because these men had been away from their families for so long they were missin their own children. I never did get the little dress clean again an afterwards somebody said to me, "Were you not worried that they might hurt your child?"

I says, "Come on, they were family men, they just loved to be wi the bairn – they only borrowed her."

A lot of people don't know we had Italian prisoners next door us you know. You hear some folk say were supposed to hate our enemies, well there was no hatred or anything wi these men.

It wasn't a secure camp, the one in Stanley, it was open, an most o the Italian prisoners worked on neighbouring farms. They could have walked out of there anytime they thought they were safe, but they didn't – I think they were quite happy to be in Stanley because they were out of the conflict. I got to know one called Guido, he was the oldest prisoner an had been taken prisoner in Abyssinia an he hadn't seen his family for about five years. Every day after the incident wi Thyrza he came round an he always had a piece of chocolate or a piece of currant cake in his top pocket an he'd come to our back door an kneel on the step beside Thyrza an she used to help herself to what he he'd brought. So that was Guido.

You'd hardly think o them as prisoners because folk in the villages speak to everyone. An when girls were passing the Italians used to call out to us. Stanley was a busy place, always something on the go, an most o the lassies worked at the mill. Some lived at home wi their families, like my sister an me, but the ones that came from other places stayed in what everybody called 'the Hen Hoose'. If you go to Stanley today you'll see the Tayside Hotel, it's all done up now – well that wis the Hen Hoose, an it was owned by the Stanley Mills, so that's where all these mill lasses stayed. Some o the local girls married Italian prisoners an (dare I say it?) one or two girls had babies they shouldn't have had. Still, that's life.

At the end of the war, when the Italian prisoners got their freedom my second baby Bob was only three weeks old. He'd had an operation an we just got him home from the hospital the day they got their freedom. Of course they were all singing at the tops o their voices, celebratin, an I says to the sergeant, "Could you ask them to be quieter?"

But you know, they shut up altogether an I said, "I didnae mean them to shut up altogether!"

An the next day they sent Paddy round to ask how the baby was. Anyway, that was the prisoners of war an of course there were big changes for everyone when the war ended in 1945.

A new life...

When Harry got demobbed, he came home to Stanley an our third baby, John, was born the following year. But the sea had been Harry's life, so he decided to go back to the fishing where he could earn a decent living an I'd be able to stay home an look after the children. We moved south, not to Hull, which is far enough away, but to Lowestoft, which is more than 500 miles from Stanley! What an upheaval that was, an there was no question o visitin my mother very often or the children havin Granny near us. But the sea was in his blood – Harry's father had been skipper on a Hull trawler though I never knew him because he had been lost at sea – we eventually found his name on a memorial to the one o the trawlers that went down with all hands: Robert Henry Hannah, skipper of the 'Amber', an the names of all his crew were listed. Hull has such a long tradition o fishin, so Harry became a deep-sea trawler man an I was a fisherman's wife.

The children were young when we moved, so it was easier for them to adjust, but for me it was a big change fae Perthshire. I missed that but I missed workin in the mill too an I don't think I ever got used to the idea o my husband bein away from home so much. I hadn't really appreciated the fact that trawlermen could be away from home for months at a time, never mind weeks. Phillip, our youngest was born in 1952 so he was used to his Dad being away for long stretches of time. We were in

Our three children, Thyrza, Robert (Bob) and John Hannah.

Lowestoft about twenty years an sometimes I felt very, very unhappy because Harry always seemed to be away. Fishin folk are maybe used to that, but I never really felt at home wi that way o life. Of course children keep you busy, an keep you goin, but there were times when I felt very lonely – I'm not sure I could ever get used to it.

The oldest children eventually left home an it was only Phillip an me, an Harry when he was home. Then I had a spell of ill-health, which dragged me down, an I probably felt more isolated than ever. My mother was still in Perthshire an my sister Margaret, who never married, had a good career in nursing. My mother used to think that my sister was the clever one of the family because she'd done all this training an had become a ward sister at Murthly Hospital. My mother lived with her an she kept house for her. It wasn't that I wanted to live wi them but I felt so unsettled, depressed really, I just felt that I need something more out of life. An I used to get *The Lady* magazine because I liked the adverts of the brilliant jobs you could get. I fantasized about getting these jobs, about getting away from the life I had. They also had cottages to let, an this day I read one that said, "Cottage to let, North East of Scotland". It was Laurencekirk, not far from Stonehaven. At the time Harry was away in Fleetwood – that was a big deep-sea fishin port till the Seventies, but it's on the west coast, so he knew nothing about this. The three older ones were all away working an Philip who was just thirteen so he was at home. But I was really unhappy just miserable, an felt there was nobody I could talk who'd understand. When I saw that ad, I was so desperate that I applied for this cottage. I got a letter back saying they were sorry I was second on the list, but a fortnight later I got another letter saying the people who had been offered it had turned it down. So it was mine, if I wished, 'sight unseen' as they said. Well I quickly got organised, filled two trunks with china an linen an before we knew it, I was on the train with Philip headin for Laurencekirk.

I've often thought that life is all about taking chances – an this was certainly one of those times. We didn't know a soul in Laurencekirk but when we got there we went to the solicitor to get the key for this tiny, little cottage in Blackmuir Avenue. The rent was thirty bob a week an it was pretty basic but it had a bathroom, it had a box bed. But it was nice enough an we soon got settled in. I didn't discover till after we'd been there a few weeks that the cottage wasn't on the main sewerage system but it had a cesspit in the back garden an it overflowed.

Philip went to the local school an not long afterwards I got friendly with the lollipop lady an I told her I needed a job. So she got me a job as a school cleaner, but I didn't like it much so she said, "Why don't you try to get a job at Stracathro Hospital as a nursing auxiliary?"

I said, "I couldn't do that. Work in a hospital? No, no I don't think so."

But she kept on about it, so I wrote to the hospital an I got a letter back saying they were sorry there was a waiting list, but if I cared to sit the entrance exam for a two year course they would be pleased to see me. I hadn't thought about doing an actual course in nursing, but I decided to go because it was only a few miles towards Brechin, about seven miles south of Laurenckirk. When I got there I nearly turned away at the gates, then I thought, "No, I'm here now."

So I went up to the Matron's office an the tutor Miss Alexander, a lovely lady, took me to the library an sat me down with a cup of coffee. She handed me a sheet of paper with thirty general knowledge questions an told me to answer as many of these questions as I could an she'd be back in twenty minutes. So I just went down the page an answered them. Miss Alexander came back an took me up to Miss Robertson in the Matron's office. She was from Aberdeen an she said, "Weel, are you pleased wi yersel?"

I said, "Should I be?"

"Yes," she told me, "you've passed with flying colours an school starts on the first of January."

At that time I was forty six an I had no school certificates, I'd nothing. It wouldn't happen now, you need a degree to do nursing. So that was a two-year course an I was the oldest in a class of about twenty-one, an it was great. The staff were wonderful an nobody treated me like an old lady an I joined in with them just like any o the student nurses.

They had a drama group so it was great to be able to

do that again, like we used to do when we were livin in Stanley. An this time we were doin 'Night Must Fall' by the Welsh playwright Emlyn Williams. It's a thriller an the matron Miss Prentice was the producer, an Billy Wallace, who worked in my ward, he was Danny the murderer an I was to play the part o the district nurse. We'd get together to rehearse for the big night an there was a scene where Danny's unconscious an I, bein the nurse, had to bring him round wi a jug of water. During rehearsals we never put any water in the jug, but on the night we put some water in the jug. An there's Danny, lying unconscious so I tilted the jug an there was water everywhere! My next line was supposed to be "It's just ten minutes since he passed out", but instead I says "It's just ten minutes since he passed away."

An Billy sat up an says, "I'm no deid yet Nell," an lay down again.

Miss Prentice wasn't pleased, an the next day there was I was being told off because it wasn't done, you know, to

Murthly Amateur Drama Group, WRI [Back row, 4th from left]

get anything wrong! Years later I went back to Stracathro for our thirty years re-union an when I went into my old ward, Ward Seven, Geriatrics, an Billy was the co-charge. An of course there was another Ward Sister with him an we were standin talkin in the ward, surrounded by old women in beds. Then without thinking I said to Billy, "Have you been murdering more old ladies, Billy?"

An the other nurse said, "What?"

"Oh I shouldn't have said that," I said, so we told her about this play we'd done all these years ago.

Nursing in Strathcathro gave me a new lease of life, it was wonderful, but I'm afraid Phillip wasn't so happy livin in Laurencekirk because he was bullied at school – some kids can be very unkind to anyone different, an it might only take one to make life miserable. Having grown up in the south, Phillip didn't speak like the rest of the kids an he used to feel like he didn't fit in. When he was in his final year he said he wanted to go to Navigational College – Aberdeen was by far the closest, but you can understan he wanted to go to Lowestoft an that was the best solution for him.

At the time I was still doing the two-year course, so I carried on at Stracathro Hospital an came out with second prize for nursing, which was quite good. So Phillip started college an I worked in Stracathro, an I loved it. It was a great hospital to work in an I'd have been happy to stay there forever. On a day off I could take the bus to visit my mother an my sister because Margaret had qualified as a psychiatric nurse an she was a ward sister at Murthly Psychiatric Hospital[29], about ten miles outside o Perth. She really enjoyed that an one day she said to me, "Why don't you come down to work here?"

Again, I didn't know how I could cope with mental

patients, because I used to see these patients going out from the hospital, they looked a bit strange to somebody who didn't know any better. Anyway she persuaded me an I came down to Murthly an had to sit another exam, a lot more stiff than the first one, an with sums in it too – I was no good at maths when I was at school an afterwards I said to my sister, "There's no way..."

But three weeks later I got a letter saying that they would employ me as a general pupil nurse until the training course started in three months time. So that was me, about to start a course in psychiatric nursing, so I moved to Murthly. I found a cottage to rent, 'Rose Cottage' – it had been vacant for quite a while an the rent was only £12 for six months. Mind you, the walls were so damp an musty an I had to scrub them for days – there was even fungus on some o them so no wonder it was so cheap! Harry would come home on leave an he'd say we'd need to get another place when he retired. Anyway, I completed the course an I was fifty two when I qualified the second time – I even got the class prize in our class

Nell's graduation day, 1969: my second nursing diploma was in Psychiatry.

o twenty, so when I was going up the steps o the City Halls to get the prize I must confess I had a great sense o satisfaction because my mother always used to say that my sister was the one wi the brains in the family, she'd had a career, while I only got married an had kids.

I enjoyed nursing at Murthly Hospital though I don't think I felt as at home there as I did at Stracathro – maybe it was because I sensed some of the nurses were guarded about what they'd tell me because they knew that the senior nurse was my sister Margaret. But every now an then we'd put on a wee show for the patients at the Murthly Hospital – everyone enjoyed that sort of thing. An I remember in Murthly we'd put on these wee shows, wi funny songs and the likes, just for a bit o fun for the patients an staff, so we'd all have a good laugh.

When my sister retired, she an my mother moved from Murthly to Perth, to Feus Road. Then one night in 1978, I'd been out at the staff social on a real wintery night, an when I got home the phone rang, really late. That was my sister Margaret phoning to tell me that my mother died – she was eighty. She was just sittin in her chair an slipped away. I carried on workin at Murthly Hospital till I retired at sixty but things didn't work out as we hoped. Sadly Harry began to suffer from Alzheimers so I nursed him until he died in 1985. It was a very difficult time for me, especially when he was in the advanced stages of the illness – but you get through it. My son John was in America, so six weeks after Harry died, I went out to see John – talk about a complete change, but it was the best thing I could have done after all the stress.

John loves music an he had a band they called 'The Infamous Grouse Band' – they sang Scottish an Irish songs. They used to get together an play in one o those

Irish pubs on a Friday night an folk get up an sing – now this was all new to me, an one night he said, "Give us a song, Mum."

"Me?" I said, "I've never sung at anything like this in my life!"

And John said, "C'm on, Mum, do your party piece!"

An I'm sayin, "The Americans won't understan a word I'm sayin!"

But anyway, I sang, an they absolutely loved it.

An believe it or not, getting up to sing in California led to another big change in my life. I met so many folk an when they asked where I sang at home, of course I said that I didna. An one o them said that, since I lived so near Perth, I should get in touch with Sheila Douglas an she'd bring me to a folk club. A Folk Club? I didn't know anything about Folk Clubs, but Sheila an Andrew had met these Americans when they used to run folksong nights at their house – they were really into the folk scene,

Visit at Universal Studios, USA

festivals everywhere, an the Americans used to love goin to the Douglas's house in Scone. So when I got home I did phone Sheila an she an Andrew started bringin me to Glenfarg Folk Club. So that's what happened.

Sheila Douglas
Photo by Aåse Goldsmith

A whole new world

I've made so many friends since the first time I went to a folk club an I've been singin ever since. Before I went to the Glenfarg club I always thought that, to sing in public you needed an accompanist, but in Glenfarg they have these singers' nights an people just get up an sing. So that's what started me – they make it so easy, and everyone gets a chance, so when it was my turn I sang. And everyone joins in the chorus so it's just such a great atmosphere.

I remember Jim Douglas was in the audience – he lives in Glenfarg, an he was an art teacher, a really good artist. I didn't know he sang because the first few times I was

Jim Douglas poet, singer and artist

there Jim sat in a corner o the audience an listened. Then one night he just stood up an began reciting, 'Last Night I Met a Morphosis'.

Everybody just fell about laughing – what talent he has. I'd no idea he was a poet as well, so that was me getting to know Jim. An during the course o some conversation I said I cam fae Turra an I must have told him about my mother an the Turra coo – usually when you say your from Turriff the first thing they say is 'Oh Turra, Turra, where else would it be but Turriff? That's the saying, an the next question is 'Dae ye ken the Turra Coo?' Anyway, one day I had a phone-call from a friend from the club an he said, "Jim's written a great song for you."

I said "What is it?"

He said, "It's ca'd 'My mither milked the Turra Coo' an it's tae the tune o 'The Red Flag'."

Nobody had ever written a song for me before, I was just delighted, so of course I learned it right away.

Jim Douglas's drawing for his song: 'My mither milked the Turra Coo'

My mither milked the Turra Coo

Ma mither knew a thing or two
When first she met the Turra Coo.
It greeted her wi friendly 'moos'
For Nellie had a wey wi coos,
An ever after she wid miss
Those balmy days o bovine bliss.
Her een wid sparkle like the dew
When she spoke o the Turra Coo.

Chorus:
Oh Turra Coo, oh Turra Coo,
We will aye remember you.
An oh, whit Ah wid gee for a coo
Like the braw wee Turra Coo.

It started wi Lloyd George's Act,
When awbody said he should be sacked
For layin oan the fermers' backs,
What they thocht wis an unfair tax.
Her owner widnae pey his due
An so they took the Turra Coo
Tae be selt at Aiberdeen
In nineteen hundred an thirteen.

But Robbie's freends aw rallied roon
An bocht the coo for fourteen poon
Before it came tae ony herm,
They took it back tae Lendrum Ferm.
An so the wee white coo cam hame,
No quite sae fleet, a wee bit lame,

But mony herts wir brimmin fu'
Tae see again the Turra Coo.

Then tourists flocked tae Turra toon;
Yid think the coo'd jumped ow'r the moon,
An they replaced their cheenie dugs
Wi Turra coos oan jars an jugs.
Tho lang since gone where guid coos go,
A land where milk an honey flow,
An jined the bull in pastures new;
We'll no forget the Turra Coo.

I was sixty-nine when I first started singin an I was over seventy when I made my first album. The girls in 'Stravaig' from Dumfries-shire did it with me – Phyllis (Martin), Susy (Kelly) and the two sisters Moira (Greenwood) and Jean

Imagine starting to sing at the age of sixty-nine! This is Stuart Duncan of Red Barn Studios – he and his wife Gillian made my albums. They've become wonderful friends to me.

(McMonies). They did all the harmonies, and you know what wonderful singers they all were, and just great fun to be with. Sadly Moira died in 2009 and she's a great loss. We recorded that cassette in 1991 at Hillside Studios Glasgow and we called it 'Nell Hannah and Friends'. Then after that there were four more, which were all recorded with Stuart and Gillian Duncan at Red Barn Studies in Perth: "It's Never Too Late" (NELL 002), "One Day At A Time" (NELL 003), "A Song for Margaret" (NELL 004), and the last CD "Young At Heart" (NELL CD 005).

It's been an amazing experience for me, first of all to make a recording at all, an then to make it four more with Gillian an Stuart Duncan from the Red Barn Studios. Theycouldn't be more helpful arranging everything, they're just wonderful. So many folk have contributed, like Anne Pack who not only sings and plays but she even wrote words for 'Margaret's Waltz' for me to sing. And when we made 'Young at Heart' in 2007 Stuart and Gillian brought the whole lot to my house an recorded the album in the livin room. I didn't think so many folk could fit in that room, but we had such fun, wi the big choruses – I can't tell you how much I've loved having these wonderful people sing with me. They've become friends for life, really – that's what you find in the folk scene, just full o special people.

Of course I recorded Jim Douglas's song about the Turra coo, an after the album came out, there was an article in the *Press and Journal* – I don't suppose they have many old age pensioners recording CDs. An there's folk all over the world who read the paper because it's a link wi home. So one day I got a letter from Canada. An I thought, "Who could be writing to me from Canada?"

Well I opened it, an it started, "Dear Mrs. Hannah, Your mother milked my father's Turra Coo…" An would you believe, this was the last surviving daughter of Robert Patterson? Well, I phoned her up in Canada an I told her that in a way I'd always been in her life because she'd heard about the coo from when she was a bairn. What happened was, that her cousin in Kintore had sent her the cutting from the *Press and Journal* an she was so desperate to get in touch that she wrote to the 'Press an Journal' an they sent it to me. It's lovely to have this link after 80 years, it's come full circle. We corresponded after that, till sadly she died. But connecting with songs an singers on the folk scene has given me so much. Suddenly parts of my life that had only belonged to the past took on a new meaning – I went back to Turra an went to the Doric Festival an in the hall was a Mr. Winton, the man who bought the farm after Mr. Patterson retired. By that time he was ninety an he was the same man who had the monument built at entrance to Lendrum Farm – it's called 'The Turra Coo Monument' an you can see it just by the road, on your way into Turriff.

The folk scene has opened up a whole new world to me, wi friends all over Scotland an everywhere else. When Sheila an Andrew couldn't take me to the Glenfarg Club, then Doris would come an collect me on a Monday evening. Other times it was Anne Park, who also plays the guitar for me. All those wonderful singers seem to know one another – you meet one or two an the next thing you know you've got so many friends who love to sing. I joined the TMSA – the Traditional Music an Song Association – they have really good festivals, where you hear the real traditional singers an players. Folk go to them year after year because it becomes like a big family reunion, wi singin an music the whole weekend.

When I first went to the Auchtermuchty Festival I was with a friend from California, Linda Brown, an she said to me, "There's a competition for female voice, why don't you enter?"

I said, "Don't be daft Linda. I'm sixty-nine!"

"Well," she said, "you're not in it to win, it's for fun."

So I decided to sing one o my mither's song 'Oh sing Tae Me the Auld Scots Sangs' but you'd to do two songs, contrasting. An somebody had given me that song 'The Egg', it's quite funny, so I sang that. The judges went away then came back an I heard my name – I'd won the cup. I couldn't believe it! I phoned my son when I came home, he said, "Were you the only contestant, Mother?"

But there I was, all these years on, singin my mither's song – I remember her singing it to me when I was a wee lassie.

Sing tae me the Auld Scots Sangs[30]

Oh sing tae me the Auld Scots sangs
In the braid auld Scottish tongue
The sangs my faither loved tae hear
The sangs my mither sang
As she sat beside my cradle
Or crooned me on her knee
An I couldnae sleep she sang sae sweet
The auld Scots sangs tae me
An I couldnae sleep, she sang sae sweet
The auld Scots sangs tae me.

Sing ony o the auld Scots sangs.
The happy or the sad

They mak me smile when I am wae.
An greet when I am glad
My hairt goes back tae auld Scotland.
The saut tears dim my e'e
An the Scotch blood leaps in a' ma' veins.
As you sing thae sangs tae me.
An the Scotch blood leaps in a' ma' veins.
As you sing thae sangs tae me.

Sing on, sing mair o thae auld sangs
For ilka ain can tell
O joy an sorrow in the past
Where mem'ries love tae dwell
Though hair grows grey an limbs grow auld,
Until the day I dee
I'll bless the Scottish tongue that sings
The auld Scots sangs tae me.

At the TMSA festivals I met Duncan Williamson an the Stewarts o Blair, Willie an Bella MacPhee, Betsy Whyte – they're full o songs an stories. An one time I was with Betsy – I think she was the first to write her own book. She was lovely, Betsy was, an I told her I'd started telling stories, just children's stories, like the ones I'd heard myself. Now, she was such a great storyteller I said to her, "I have a nerve thinking I can tell stories!"

But Betsy said to me, "I love your stories, Nell, why don't you tape them an practise them like that?" She gave me that encouragement so in September I went to Kirriemuir Folk Festival an I won the cup for storytelling. I told a version o 'The Wee Bannock'. So that same year I'd the two cups on my mantelpiece, but like my friend Linda said, it's not about the winnin, it's about the fun everyone has. There's great sing-arounds an everybody can join in.

Once I'd started singin I discovered I had hundreds o songs. I must have listened when I was small an just took them in like a sponge. An gettin a chance to sing them gives you the confidence then to learn new ones, songs that catch your fancy – I still hear new songs I'd like to learn. In fact the last time I was in California visiting my song John, his band members surprised him one day by singing to him a song that he'd composed – he'd written the words of 'One Spare Kiss' and Yvonne McLeod wrote the tune for it – she's a lovely accordionist and musician. Then to surprise him the band all learned it and sang it to him. So I sing it now – in fact it's on my last album, 'Young at Heart'.

One Spare Kiss[31]

One spare kiss is all I ask,
One touch of lips you'd surely dare
One spare kiss is all I'd need
To know you must still care.

That night long ago on the banks of the Tay
There were kisses like stars falling round
   where we lay
Now millions of kisses I'd gladly would pay
For one spare kiss of thine.

One spare kiss is all I ask,
One touch of lips you'd surely dare
One spare kiss is all I would need
To know you would still care.

You lay in my arms till the sun rose anew
Then we walked hand in hand through
   the sparkling dew
Now our love has grown old
   and that love it was true
Has gone like those kisses of thine.

One spare kiss is all I ask,
One touch of lips you'd surely dare
One spare kiss is all I would need
To know you must still care.

Now love ebbs and flows like the swing of the tide
And like sunshine in winter will never long bide
But your lips alone would stop time and its stride
With one spare kiss of thine,

One spare kiss is all I ask,
One touch of lips you'd surely dare
One spare kiss is all I'd need
To know you could still care.

You somehow get the same feeling about poems and recitations and stories. Some o the stories are true, an folk get talkin about things that happened them. You'll remember Big Willie MacPhee an Bella, his wife. Lovely couple they were and Willie was a fantastic storyteller. But there was one time we all got invited to Balquhidder, way down the loch where Rob Roy was born. The drive along this one track-road was adventure in itself and we had a great ceilidh and we all stayed the night. Imagine doing that sort of thing in your seventies! Willie and I talked about it afterwards – we would 't have missed it despite the windy road there!

Through the folk scene I've met so many folk an had some wonderful experiences. I've met some quite famous folk too – Billy Connolly, Barbara Dickson, Hamish Imlach, the McCalmans, Paddie Bell who used to sing wi the Corries – I sang with her at the Edinburgh Fringe. And of course that's where I met Nancy Nicolson – she's a wonderful song-writer and everybody loves Nancy. This is one of her more serious songs, written after the awful disaster in the North Sea:

Nancy Nicolson & Pino Mereu, 15 November 2008

Who Pays The Piper?[32]

Chorus:
Who pays the piper, who pays the piper?
Who pays the piper, who calls the tune?
Who pays the piper, what is the fee?
Flames on the water, death on the sea.

And the tune is old and has always told
How the great brave and bold they do flourish;
How bravely they gamble with other men's lives
And profit as other men perish.

And the tune rings out and is always found
When the ground receives yet another
Father of dazed and despairing young bairns
Or son of a desolate mother.

And the price is dear for the folk who fear
And who bear the burden of sorrow
For those who were lost when the graph
   of the cost
Crossed the graph of rich pickings tomorrow

Then, of course there was Danny Kyle – he used to go to Glenfarg, which is probably where I first met him. He was at lots o festivals and just great fun to be with. I remember one time I went to a Folk Night at the Dundee Rep and Danny Kyle was the compere and Annie Watkins was booked to sing. You'll remember Annie – I think she was over seventy – a real character and she had an amazing voice. And I mind when it was her turn to go on stage Danny had announced her and she didn't come on. And Danny's looking round wondering where's Annie. And there she was, sitting at the side o the stage eatin fish an chips! Now if you didn't know what to expect, this wee wifie gettin up to sing, you'd be in for a surprise – she really could sing and she sometimes used to get the Foundry Bar Band to play wi her. And the first song I heard her sing was this one – I just fell in love with it so I've been singin it ever since. It's on my last CD:

Bonnie Wee Lochee Lass[33]

It fell upon a Lammas nicht
When I went oot for a stroll,
I hadna been sae very far
When I wandered doon by the toll,
I'd only gaed a mile or twa
When a bonnie fair I did pass,
'Twas there I fell in love
Wi my bonnie wee Lochee Lass.

Chorus
"Now whaur are ye gaun?
Gimme yer haun, hoo dae ye dae?" says I,
"Haud up yer heid ma bonnie wee lass,
now dinna be sae shy,
Whaur dae ye stye? Whaur dae ye bide?
Come tell tae me yer name,
Wid yer faither no be angry noo
if I wis tae see ye hame?"

We stood, we cracked a guid lang while
aboot a thing or twa,
We werena thinkin o the time
till the stars had gaed awa,
She drew her shawl aroon her heid
an quietly she did explain,
"Ye'll need tae keep yer word, young man,
for ye promised tae see me hame."

Chorus
"Now whaur are ye gaun?

An now we both are mairrit
an as happy as we can be,
She's got twa bairnies by her side,
another een on her knee,
We sit an crack at oor fireside
an think o the times that have passed,
I'll never forget the nicht I fell
in love wi ma Lochee Lass.

Chorus
"Now whaur are ye gaun?

When Danny started doin his Open Stage (at Celtic Connections Festival in Glasgow) he gave so much encouragement to folk who'd sing or play. He was a terrific singer an guitarist himself an a fantastic MC – that's how I got to know him. Danny gave so much to his Open Stage an when I went up to sing he used to go on an say, "The next woman that's comin' on is the sexiest woman I've ever met."

An I'd walk on an say "What a disappointment!" So I'd sing one, and I'd usually choose something funny, because once the audience catch on it's just great fun.

Bein a part o the folk scene has brought me into contact wi so many folk I'd never dreamed o meetin. It keeps me goin an since my sister Margaret died of Alzheimer's, like Harry, I started doin charity concerts to support Alzheimer's Scotland. Folk just rally round an it's wonderful. Sometimes when I'm with other folk who are gettin up in years an there's aye something up wi us, for a laugh I recite this wee poem:

How do I know my youth is well spent?
Well, my get up an go, just got up an went.
I don't really mind, as I think with a grin,
Of all the grand places my 'get up' has been.
Old age is golden, I've heard it said,
But sometimes I wonder when I get into bed
With my hearing aid in a drawer
An my teeth in a cup,
My specs on the table in case I get up.
Ere sleep comes to me
I think to myself, "Is there anything else
I should have left on the shelf?"
I get up each morning, dust off my wits
Pick up the paper an read the obits
If my name is still missing I know I'm not dead
So I have a good breakfast an go back to bed.

One o the things that has given me greatest pleasure in the past few years is organising charity concerts – I'm sayin 'organising' but really it's my wonderful friends who make sure it all comes together. Then I invite everyone I think will come and on the night it's great to see everyone. My last concert was the Jubilee Concert, for the Queen's Diamond Jubilee in 2012, which was very close to my ninety-second birthday. It was held in the Souter Theatre in the A.K. Bell Library in Perth and the place was packed. And what a line-up of singers and musicians! There was Gillian and Stewart Duncan, Anne Parke, Jim Douglas, Donald Innes, Margaret Bennett, Linda Dewar, Jess Smith, Claire Hewitt, Phillip Hannah, Betsy Smith, two lovely children called Blair and Morgan as well as Heather Innes, Ciaran Dorris and Kate Kramer. What a night we had!

This is a group from the Royal Conservatoire of Scotland who visited Nell in Perth: L to R: Sarah MacNeill, Imogen Poropat, Nell, Ainsley Hamill and Robyn Stapleton. And they're all wonderful musicians and singers.

I've really enjoyed goin back to the Stanley Mills an speakin to groups, clubs, an school children. Folk could read books about the mill, but meetin someone who actually worked there is different. An since goin back I've learned a few more songs about workin in the mill – this one is by Mary Brooksbank who worked in a jute mill in Dundee. She worked there before my time but I can just imagine what it was like for this lassie:

The Jute Mill Song[34]

Oh, dear me, the mill's gaen fest,
The puir wee shifter canna get a rest.
Shiftin bobbins, coorse an fine,
They fairly mak ye work for yer ten an nine.

Oh, dear me, I wish the day wis done,
Rinnin up an doon the pass is no nae fun;

Shiftin, piecin, spinnin warp, weft an twine,
Tae feed an cled my bairnie affen ten an nine

Oh, dear me, the warld's ill divided,
For them that wark the hardest are wi
    least provided,
But I'll jist bide contentit, dark days or fine,
But there's no much pleasure living
    affen ten an nine.

An mind I said that I would look out o the window at the river, that lovely view fae the Stanley Mill? Well, it was that sort o thing that saved you on days that were dreary. It's so beautiful an it could take your mind off other things.

When I first heard Ewan McVicar's song, 'Shift an Spin' I really took to that song an that's another one that has everyone joinin the chorus:

Ewan McVicar

Shift an Spin

Chorus:
Shift an spin, warp an twine
Making thread coarse an fine
Dreamin o yer valentine
Workin in the mill

Keep yer bobbins runnin easy
Show ye're gallus, bright an breezy
Waitin till Prince Charmin sees ye
Workin in the mill

Oil yer runners, mend yer thread
Do yer best until you're dead
You wish you were a wife instead o
Workin in the mill

Used to dream you'd be the rage
Smilin on the fashion page
Never dreamt you'd be a wage slave
Workin in the mill

Used to think that life was kind
No it isn't, never mind
Maybe some day love will find you
Workin in the mill

He loves you not? So what?
Make the best of what you've got
Win your pay, spin your cotton
Workin in the mill.

An talk o Prince Charming! I'll never forget the day of the official opening of the Stanley Mill after it was refurbished as a museum. It had been closed since 1989 an it was nearly demolished but then Prince Charles got involved – he's got a real passion for heritage buildings an one of the very first projects funded by Prince's Regeneration Trust was Stanley Mill Museum. He had visited the mill in 1997, before Historic Scotlan began the restoration so he really did know the state it was in.[35] Then when it was opened in June 2010, folk who'd worked at the mill were invited – they wanted to have the ones who'd been there in the 1940s an the Rural ladies were practising their curtsy. I said, "Oh my, have I got to curtsy? If I get doon I winna get up again!" When he arrived at the mill wi John Swinney, Prince Charles was in the kilt, Hunting Stewart tartan, an he was wearing the most beautiful, blue wool socks. When we were introduced to him, he said he was glad that three of us got seats – he noticed that an he couldn't have been nicer to us. You can even see it on Youtube[36], an you can see him shaking hands wi us! It was such a special day – I wonder what my mother would have thought, her daughter meeting royalty?

This was taken when Prince Charles visited the Stanley Mills Museum and those of us who had worked there during the war were invited to meet him. It was a really wonderful day and he was so friendly, talking to us all.

It's over seventy years since my mother an my sister Margaret an I came to Stanley. Lookin back I love talkin to folk about what it was like at the mill. For school-children especially, they can imagine exactly what it was like an they can ask questions an I can teach them the songs an choruses. There's just so many stories to tell – ma mither said I was vaccinated with a gramophone needle! I think she might have been right, but the world would be a gey poor place wi nae songs or stories. I've got such a lot to be thankful for an I've made the most wonderful friends through songs an singin.

Paddie Bell

A night with friends, Perth 2012.

Looking Back...

Here are some newspaper cuttings from my collection – I can look back with huge gratitude to all those who have shared these moments with me. They have brought untold pleasure not only to me but also to so many others. I'd like to say a huge thank you to all of you!

Nell (78) hits a high note with follow-up album

Busking for Alzheimers

Nell Hannah (centre) from Perth launched her fourth album at a concert in the West End Bowling Club. The album, A Song For Margaret, was produced in memory of her sister. With Nell are singer Anne Pack, producer Stuart Duncan of Red Barn Studios, Provost Mike O'Malley, backing singer Gillian Murray and Kate O'Malley.

Awards for improving quality of life of others

By Mike Donachie

CONTRIBUTIONS to improving the quality of life of older people in Perth and Kinross were celebrated last night.

Part of the local events for the International Year of the Older Person, the Celebration of Age event in Perth City Halls was hosted by Scottish entertainer Jimmy Logan and Perth and Kinross Provost Mike O'Malley.

Ten deserving locals received awards for their work on behalf of older people, after being nominated in six categories.

The show included performances by the Julie Young Dancers, Perthshire Brass, pianist and singer Mike Ellacott, the Perth Strathspey and Reel Society and singer and storyteller Nell Hannah, herself a prize winner.

Before it began the provost said, "I know this will be an excellent show and I would like to thank everyone involved.

"Thanks to the performers for giving their time to bring enjoyment to so many people once again, and to Jimmy Logan for ably taking on the role of our MC for the evening, to the team who have organ-

ised the awards and the celebration and everyone who has been nominated or has nominated someone.

"It just goes to show that we have a lot of unsung heroes out there, and I hope that in this way we can recognise their efforts," he added.

Awards:

Social care (over-50): Mrs Sylvia Duthie, for her work in

Back—entertainer Henry Neil, Bob Jardine, James Whyte, David Miller, Nell Hannah and Margaret Gray; front—Sylvia Duthie, Annie Bell, Mike O'Malley, Jean Dickson, Harry Ruthven, Margaret Myles, Jimmy Logan.

setting up and running the Perth and Perthshire Fund for the Elderly.

Social care (under-50): David Miller, for his help with the VISOR group, which offers support and activities for the visually impaired.

Recreation, education and entertainment: two awards.

Annie Bell, who has spent a lifetime entertaining with songs, accordion-playing and poetry—and continues to do so, despite severe arthritis.

Nell Hannah, who has recorded two albums of songs and stories and brings pleasure to many people of all ages, having taken up music after the death of her husband.

Fitness and health: a joint award to Jean Dickson and Margaret Gray, for their commitment to running an exercise class for older people in the Dunkeld area.

Citizenship: two awards.

Harry Ruthven, for his dedicated work towards the develop-

ment of Bowerswell Memorial Homes in Perth. Bob Jardine, for his efforts in helping establish 50-Plus Forum groups throughout Perth and Kinross.

Volunteering: two awards.

James Whyte, for his work with older people at the Lewis Place Resource Centre in Perth, supporting their craft activities through his skills in the centre's joinery workshop.

Margaret Myles, for more than 20 years' voluntary service in Crieff.

Biographic Notes

MARGARET BENNETT

Margaret Bennett is a folklorist, writer, singer and broadcaster who comes from a family of tradition bearers, Gaelic on her mother's side (from Skye) and Lowland Scots on her father's.

As a student inspired by folklorist Hamish Henderson, she studied Folklore and since the late Sixties has been recording and writing about Scottish tradition, as well as singing and storytelling. From 1984 to 1996 she lectured at The University of Edinburgh's School of Scottish Studies and now teaches part-time at the Royal Conservatoire of Scotland. Based in Perthshire, she is a Trustee of 'Grace Notes Scotland', a Scottish Charity dedicated to handing on traditions to new generations.

DORIS ROUGVIE

Born in Pitcairngreen in rural Perthshire where music and songs were a vital part of daily life, Doris has always had a great passion for singing. She is a regular guest at festivals and folk clubs around Scotland both as a soloist and as part of the duo 'Wildfire' with her long time singing partner Brenda Frier. Doris is equally at home singing traditional and contemporary material and her clear tones and soaring voice never fail to leave the listener moved by her performance. Doris has won many trophies for traditional singing and is an avid festival goer.

Doris is in her element sharing songs with others and is the popular host of 'The House of Song' at various festivals and events including Celtic Connections, Orkney Folk Festival and the Scots Trad Awards.

Doris is a central figure on the Scottish folk scene, and has been awarded Life Membership of the Traditional Music and

Song Association of Scotland, for whom she has organised concerts, workshops and other events. Doris was also granted Life Membership of Glenfarg Village Folk Club having finally relinquished her position as Publicity Officer after 30+ years.

Doris was co-author with Margaret of two earlier books – *'Then another thing – Remembered in Perthshire' (1999)* and *'In our day – Reminiscences and songs from rural Perthshire' (2010)*. Doris is a talented artist and provided the illustrations for both these previous books as well as the present one.

Endnotes

1. The Australian and New Zealand Army Corps (which also included soldiers from the Cook Island, Niue, Samoa and Tonga) joined the First World War in 1915. Their National holiday, ANZAC Day, observed on April 25, commemorates the horrific slaughter, as well as outstanding bravery, of soldiers who fought at Gallipoli. Nell's father was among the survivors.

2. Robert Burns wrote the song in 1786 for a young woman he noticed while wandering in the grounds of Balochmyle House. Though known now by its popular title (or sometimes by 'The Lass o Ballochmyle'), the original manuscript bears no title, but simply an inscription: 'A Song -- Tune Etrick banks -- On accidentally seeing Miss W.–" The young lady was Wilhelmina Alexander who happened to be visiting her brother Claud, owner of the estate. The original song has five 8 line verses, while the one that has become a household favourite has three. As it begins on verse 3, the opening verses (or index-related first line) may not be familiar to those who sing the song. For over a century it has been a concert favourite among Scots all over the world as it was recorded on 78 rpm records as early as 1911 by American tenor John Jamieson (Columbia-Rena records).

3. Sometimes called 'Bonnie Mary of Argyle', the song appears in several collections from the mid-to late 1800s though it first appeared as a Broadside ballad, entitled 'Bonny Mary', printed in Glasgow by James Lindsay, c. 1860. (The National Library of Scotland)

The lyrics were composed around 1850 by Charles Jeffrey who was inspired by the story of Robert Burns and his 'Highland Mary' (Mary Campbell, 1763-1786), who died tragically young. Jeffrey's collaborated was fellow Englishman S. Nelson who composed the melody to suit the words and it soon became a concert favourite recorded on 78 rpm discs by the likes of John McCormack (1914) and Heddle Nash (1931). Interestingly, 'Mary Of Argyle; was also Side B of John Jamieson's 1911 recording of 'The Bonnie Lass Of Ballochmyle'. (Roud number 12904)

4. The song was composed by Johnny Patterson (1840-89) from County Clare who was a singer, song-writer and circus entertainer. While he became famous on both sides of the Atlantic during his life for his performances as well as song compositions, the age of recording had not quite arrived. As a result, later singers such Josef Locke, John McCormack and others who recorded his song became better known than Patterson.

5. Also known as 'Andrew Lammie' or 'The Trumpeter of Fyvie', the ballad is in the collection of Francis James Child, Number 233. See, *The English and Scottish Popular Ballads*, Vol. 4. (Roud number 98)

6. Liberal politician David Lloyd George led a series of radical social reforms and is credited for laying the foundation of Britain's welfare state. A Welshman, whose second language was English, he was Chancellor of the Exchequer at the time of this incident and was Prime Minister from 1916 to 1922. As he was leader of the Liberal Party from 1926 to 1931 and continued in politics until 1942, for Nell's generation he was a very familiar figure in British Politics.

7. The 48-line poem is by no means identical to the original composition, as there were several lines that Nell could not quite complete. She could, however, recall the individuals named and tell why they were memorable. As we have not been able to trace a printed version to help fill in the missing words, I have adapted her detailed information to complete lines 20 to 48. As Nell remembered so many of the characters and more than half the poem, I felt it would be a shame to miss it out because it was incomplete. I admit responsibility for lapses in the style and hope that readers will excuse any errors they find. If anyone finds an 'original', we will be delighted to receive a copy and replace this with the complete version of the original composition. (MB)

8. Traditional, in several collections including Norman Buchan, *101 Scottish Songs*, Glasgow, 1962, pp. 76-77; Gavin Greig, *Folk-Song of the North-East* (reprint edition, by K. Goldstein and A. Argo, Hotboro, PA, 1963; article CLXXVI; and *Greig-Duncan Folk Song Collection*, edited by Patrick Shuldham-Shaw & Emily Lyle, Aberdeen Univ. Press & EUP) Vol. 1, pp. 178-179, song number 77.

9. The song was a popular party piece for children over fifty years ago, as I recall my aunt teaching my sisters and me to sing it, and to do the actions. I have no idea, however, where it started off. (MB)

10. Gavin Greig, better known as a song collector, was the playwright who penned the Doris series of dramatic sketches based on life at The Mains. His best known piece was play, The Mains Wooin (c. 1910).

11. This may be from a much longer traditional ballad of the same title as the verses sung here are very

similar to some of the old ballad (Roud 16143). It may be impossible to verify but it seem likely that the old song was cut down for the 78 rpm recording as these discs could only play approximately 3 minutes, so it was very common for songs to be truncated. Though Nell does not remember who sang the version she first heard, it ma have been the American cowboy singer Carson Robison who sometimes sang under the name of Bud Billings – he released both songs as Sides A and B on a 78 rmp disc in 1925.

12. In today's money, 25 pence.

13. Traditional; widely differing variants published in well-known collections such as John Ord, *Bothy Songs & Ballads*, Glasgow, 1930, pp. 214-215; N. Buchan, *101 Scottish Songs*, pp. 36-37; *Folk-Song of the North-East* (G. Greig, K. Goldstein & A. Argo) article IV; *Greig-Duncan* vol. 3, pp. 3-9; W. Kemp & J. S. Kerr, *Kerr's Cornkisters*, 1950, pp. 29-30. (Roud number 2136)

14. Composed by George Smith Morris (1876 – 1958) from Aberdeen, who was a singer and writer of comic song in Doric, the song was published in Kerr's *Buchan Bothy Ballads* Vol. 2 (1957) pp. 2-3 and Norman Buchan, *101 Scottish Songs* 1960, pp. 48-49. (Roud 1875)

15. Composed by George Bruce Thomson, the song is published in *Greig-Duncan* vol. 3, pp. 508-510 and in Norman Buchan, *Scottish Ballad Book*, Glasgow, 1973, pp. 204-206. (Roud number 2518)

16. Willie Kemp (1888–1965) from Oldmeldrum became known as the 'King o the Cornkisters' as he made a name for himself composing the melodies of

several popular songs in Doric, co-written with George Bruce Thomson and others. In the 1920s his BBC broadcasts led to a recording contract with Beltona Records, with whom he continued to record throughout the 1930s. His sister Agnes Kemp married George S. Morris and after the marriage (1912), they moved to Oldmeldrum, then, for several years Morris collaborated with his brother-in-law Willie Kemp and also recorded for Beltona Records. All three leave a significant legacy of popular north-east songs.

17. Composed by George S. Morris.

18. Bankfoot is eight miles north of Perth and seven miles south of Dunkeld.

19. Originally set up as a cotton mill (the furthest north in Britain), from 1921 it operated as a jute mill, and was linked to the jute trade in Dundee.

20. A wage of two pounds fifteen shillings (usually written £2/15/0) is £2.75 in modern UK currency.

21. Cotton mill workers in the American south used the same terms. See James Leloudis and Kathryn Walber, *Like a Family: The Making of a Southern Cotton Mill World*, Chapel Hill (University of North Carolina Press), 1987, interviews with mill workers for an oral history project in North Carolina, p. 4.

22. Like many of her generation, Nell first heard the song on the wireless, following the successful WW2 movie, 'The Way to the Stars' in which it was sung by 16 year-old Jean Simmons. (The movie starred John Mills, Michael Redgrave and Stanley Holloway and Jean Simmons.) The song is traditional, however,

and originates in Ireland where it has several variants, many of which were sent to Sam Henry in 1933. See, 'Adieu to cold winter' and other titles under H504, published in G. Huntington and Lani Herrmann, *Sam Henry's Songs of the People*, p. 347. (Roud number 1034)

23. Professional actors Marjory Dense and David Steuart founded Perth Theatre in 1935. Both had been members of the Lena Ashwell Players, the first theatre company to produce large-scale entertainment for the troops during World War I and were committed to making high culture available to 'ordinary people'.

24. Originally written in 1881 by Norwegian playwright Henrik Ibsen, the play deals with moral issues seldom mentioned in his day. The English version shocked audiences all over the world when it was premiered.

25. Traditional. (Roud number 387)

26. Utility clothing was introduced in response to the shortage of materials during the war. Fashions changed as a result of short supplies and there were strict specification in the clothing industry, producing, for example, knee length skirts were with a limited number of pleats limited, single-breasted jackets, and trims such as lace. The rules also applied to household linen and furnishings and all items carried a Utility label, CC41, which stands for 'civilian clothing'.

27. Less than a pound for the food bill – 80 pence fed 18 people.

28. Charles's father, James Francis Edward Stuart, (known as 'The Old Pretender') was married to Countess Maria Klementyna Sobieska, grand-daughter of King Sobieski III of Poland.

29. Opened in 1854 and originally named 'Perth District Asylum', this was the second purpose-built hospital to open in Scotland in response to the Scottish Act of 1857 requiring local authorities to proved care for 'pauper lunatics'. The emphasis was on therapeutic occupation and exercise and there was a farm as well as facilities to teach sewing and other crafts. It closed in 1985 and the building was demolished.

30. Traditional. Published in *The Morwen Collection of Scottish Songs*, with accompaniments for piano, Glasgow (Mozart Allan), 1895, p. 202.

31. Composed by John Hannah and recorded by Nell, trach 13 on her CD ' Young at Heart' (NELLCD 005), Red Barn Studios, 2007.

32. Nancy composed the song after the 1988 Piper Alpha disaster when an explosion and fire on the North Sea oil rig killed 167 men. Of the 226 who worked on the rig, only 59 survived.

33. Nell's version is very close to the song Annie Watkins sang to Peter Shepheard who recorded her (Springthyme Records), published in Songs and Ballads of Dundee by Nigel Gatherer (#65). Though this version of the song is localised to Lochee in Fife, there are variants from other parts of Scotland such Willie Scott's song from the Borders, 'The Bonnie Wee Trampin Lass' (see *Herd Laddie o the Glen*, pp. 80–81, where the lass is a mill-worker.) It appears to have been popular among farm workers and may have arrived via seasonal workers from Northern

Ireland as it was very popular there in the early Thirties. Several version were sent to Sam Henry in 1933 to be published in his weekly song column in *The Northern Constitution* – he received a version from Carrickfergus with title 'The Bonny Wee Lass', and two more with same title as Willie Scott: 'The Bonnie Wee Trampin Lass', one from Balnamore, Co. Antrim and one from Limavady, Co. Londonderry. (See, G. Huntington and Lani Herrmann, *Sam Henry's Songs of the People*, p. 459).

34. Mary's own Dundee pronunciation was also what she published in her poetry collection, *Sidlaw Breezes* (Dundee, 1966) Subsequent publications have changed it to 'fast' which does not rhyme with 'rest'. (Roud number 2585)

35. Partner funders included the Gannochy Trust, Architectural Heritage Fund, Heritage Lottery Fund, and Artefact Conservators.

36. The piece, titled 'Stanley Mills: Preserving Scotland's Heritage', is attributed to the Royal channel. It takes in some of the speeches, key people (including Nell), and general views of the Stanley Mill. See: https://www.youtube.com/watch?v=YzK34gXuc_s&feature=player_embedded.

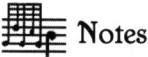 Notes

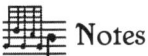 Notes

 Notes

 Notes

4624737R00081

Printed in Great Britain
by Amazon.co.uk, Ltd.,
Marston Gate.